The Christian Journey

Part Two

All Scripture quotations are taken from the Holy Bible,
New King James Version (NKJV).

Cover and pagination created by Kate Bittner.

dorishoman@gmail.com
www.myjoyandcrown.wordpress.com

Preface

Your amazing spiritual journey continues in **The Christian Journey** : Part Two. There is nothing more life changing than following the road map laid out for us in the Bible. **The Christian Journey** is a discipleship study for those who have placed their trust in Jesus Christ and desire to grow in the fundamentals of the Christian faith.

The objective of this study is to teach God's plan for mankind and build on the knowledge of the Word of God, the Bible by teaching such topics as how to share your faith, determining your spiritual gifts and how to use them, understanding spiritual warfare and how to be prepared, and many more key topics.

The Christian Journey is a great study guide for one-on-one discipleship, bible study, small groups or a Sunday school class. In the back you will find a list of terms and definitions to aid in your understanding as you study. New King James Version (NKJV) is used.

Before we get started, I want to share with you my story and journey of faith (that I shared in Book One). I was born in Cairo, Egypt, in a very strict religious environment. I grew up attending church and loved Sunday school as a child. My grandfather told us Bible stories; his example gave me a love for God. I desired to know God but somehow He seemed far. At the age of 9 my family and I moved to the US. It was a difficult time of transition for me. Finding myself in a foreign land with no extended family and no friends; I struggled with loneliness and a sense of not belonging for many years.

A couple of important things happened in my teen years; I was invited to attend an evangelical church and around the same time, some friends from high school asked me to attend Campus Crusade meetings. I began to attend both regularly and for the first time in my life I heard that I could have a relationship with God and know Him personally. This was amazing and a defining moment for me. This is what I really had desired all along, not religion but a relationship!

I struggled for a while as I felt I was already a believer in Christ but one evening, after church, I remember sitting in my room and talking to God. I acknowledged my faith in Him and my desire to have a relationship with Him. I turned leadership of my life over to Him to transform me into the person He intended me to be. (Proverbs 3:5-6)

Slowly I began to study the Bible, pray and grow in my relationship with Christ. Over time, I began to see many changes in my life. Christ took a very shy and insecure girl and transformed her into someone He can use to initiate and reach out to others. I never thought I could stand before a group of people and speak, let alone prepare lessons and teach the Bible. He gave me a purpose and a mission. (Galatians 2:20)

During my college years I met my husband and a year later, we got married. In my thirties, the Lord began to stir in me a real desire for teaching the Bible to women. I had the opportunity to attend several training seminars by Precept Ministries and through the inductive study method, I learned how to study, prepare and lead Bible studies.

God has given me a heart for women and a passion to see them established in His Word and using their spiritual gifts in service for Him in their local church. For the past 20 years I have lead women's Bible Studies, 6 years leading women's Sunday school class as well as small group. It's been a joy to work in women's ministries side by side with other women of faith.

Soon after a Bible Study series on the Names of God, one of our ladies was diagnosed with cancer and went through a long period of treatment and recovery. I will never forget when she told me that if it wasn't for the Names of God study we had just completed, her faith would not have been as strong during this storm in her life.

Another important part of women's ministries is developing future leaders. I am passionate about seeing women grow into future teachers and leaders so they can train other women on their journey with Christ. (II Timothy 2:2)

A few years ago I saw a need for this curriculum; material that covers the basic aspects of the Christian life all in one study guide. This study you are about to dive into is the culmination of the last 35 years of my walk with Christ. It is important as a follower of Christ to know what we believe and why we believe it. It is my heart's desire and goal that this curriculum will have an impact in women's lives and firmly establish them in the scriptures. It is one thing to read the Bible and another thing to study it; to dig deeper. I have often said to my ladies that the Word of God is like a mine; the more we dig the more treasure we will find.

This journey has taken over 6 years to compile with numerous revisions. I had the opportunity to take a group of about 20 women through this study after which many more revisions followed as I saw areas for improvement.

About 4 years after writing this material, God brought Davia Rinehart into my life through a mutual friend. Davia has been engaged in discipling women (disciples of Christ) for many years. Living about 500 miles away, she graciously came to Cincinnati to meet with me several times. I am so grateful for how she has invested of herself in this project. I am indebted to her for the hours she has spent reviewing the curriculum and hours of meeting with me with her suggestions and recommendations; her godly perspective and insight enriched this material.

I am also thankful to Sue Neumann and Mike Marker. Their feedback and edits greatly improved this study.

Foreword

When a person makes the decision to follow Jesus Christ, that moment marks the beginning of a life filled with incredible opportunities – or the beginning of chronic disappointments. Even those of us who claim to know Him still fall asleep each night, only to wake the next morning having forgotten who we are, and who God really is. We need a foundation of Biblical truth, a community of pursuant believers, and encouragement to continue growing in our faith. If we don't have these things, we find ourselves disillusioned and discouraged, wondering what it is we are doing in the first place. We lose sight of the goal – an intimate relationship with God, ourselves, and others.

What I love about Doris' **The Christian Journey** is that the basics are covered – and we are encouraged to keep moving forward. Having had the privilege of knowing Doris for several years, I've seen her devotion to Christ and her passion to see others stand firm in their commitment to Him. Whether you are a young believer just beginning your faith journey or have walked with God many years, this resource is for you. At Greater Impact Ministries, we are excited to see this new resource and are happy to help get the word out.

I have recommended this material for one-on-one discipleship with other women, helping them understand and grow in their new found faith. We are eager for you to experience God on a deeper level with each passing year, so whether you are revisiting the basics or using the basics to help others lay a solid foundation for their faith in Christ, you will find this study guide extremely useful. We are pleased to list this material among our Titus 2 Women's Leadership Resources.

Enjoy the journey, and remember there is no condemnation in Christ Jesus – only more opportunities for intimacy with Him!

Nina Roesner
Author
The Respect Dare: 40 Days to a Deeper Connection with God and Your Husband (Thomas Nelson, 2012)
With All Due Respect: 40 Days to a More Fulfilling Relationship with Your Teens and Tweens (Thomas Nelson, 2016), Trainer, and Speaker.
12 Truths to Change Your Marriage (Greater Impact Publishing, 2012)
Daughters of Sarah: A Training Course for Wives (Greater Impact Publishing, 2012)
Executive Director, Greater Impact Ministries, Inc.

I first met Doris in church a few years ago. We actually sat two rows apart on Sunday mornings for quite some time before we even spoke. I was drawn to her; I knew she was different—a strong believer. She glowed as she worshipped Him.

New to the church my husband and I were invited to a small group. Was it simply a coincidence that it was Doris co-leading the study? I sat spellbound as I watched her answer questions, provide biblical references, and point us in the right direction on the challenging topic of the end times. When there were opposing views, she listened and promised to do more research. The next week she followed through, teaching from historical knowledge as well as biblical reference.

Doris and I quickly became friends. Over coffee, I shared with her the work Nina Roesner and I (and many others) were doing at Greater Impact Ministries, which focuses its ministry on marriage and family. Our vision is also directed towards training women to become Titus 2 leaders. Doris then shared with me the bible study she had written several years prior.

Others had also mentioned her study. I knew it was a divine appointment; with one look at the material, I knew it was what our ministry needed to help women get established in their faith.

Often times in ministry we encounter women who have knowledge of Jesus Christ but don't necessarily understand how to incorporate Him into their daily lives. They don't have a full understanding of whether they have eternal salvation, or what it means to be a Christian. That is where this study comes in. We have since used this study many times with new believers. It's basic, yet powerful. It will take you through the essentials of what it means to be a Christ follower.

Grab your Bibles, grab some friends, and start learning all you can about your walk with a living God!

Debbie Hitchcock
Author, *With All Due Respect* (Thomas Nelson, 2016),
Trainer, and Speaker
Operations Director, Greater Impact Ministries, Inc.

You've heard a word from God. You've opened your heart and asked Him to come in to live inside. For the first time in your life you feel truly alive. Questions are populating your mind. What next? What do I do? How do I live? What must I change? How do I know I am walking in truth? Am I seeking to know and understand the true and living God? What does He want from me and how can I serve Him well?

In this study guide Doris Homan walks readers through the biblical principles so eloquently laid out in God's Word so that they can truly live a life of freedom in Him.

For the last 25 years, I've had the privilege of knowing Doris Homan as a bible teacher and friend. Her knowledge of

God's Word has always inspired me. Over the years she's demonstrated herself as a phenomenal women's ministry leader, has escorted women to the throne of grace by leading and teaching countless bible studies and weekly Sunday School classes, led a women's small group ministry, spoke at women's events and served one-on-one as a mentor, Christian counselor and discipler. I've witnessed first-hand the need for discipleship and was not surprised that Doris would write a study ministering to that need. She was able to write it because she has lived it. Her desire to serve God and to help others know Him by growing deeper in their faith is evident in all that she does.

As you go through this study, you will be digging deep into the scriptures God has laid out for us in His Word. Why? So that you can see for yourself the truth of God and how His Word comes alive when you diligently seek Him. The end result will be a personal faith that is based upon a true and intimate relationship with your creator. Further manifestation of this personal growth is you won't be able to keep it to yourself! You will become a light to all you encounter, thus fulfilling your sole purpose on this earth ... ***to love God and to love people.***

You shall love the Lord your God with all your heart, with all your soul, and with all your mind. This is the first and great commandment. And the second is like it: 'You shall love your neighbor as yourself.' Matthew 22:37-40.

Walking in the way of the Lord can be encompassed in these verses. Discipling others to do the same is a calling that God has given each of us who know Him.

As you grow in your faith and in the knowledge of the One who created you and loves you beyond measure, may you find His peace and abundant mercy.

Cindy Kreis
Women's Ministries

The Christian Journey

Part Two

Second Coming: How can I be prepared

Appendix

Glossary

RELATIONSHIPS:

HOW SHOULD I RESPOND TO OTHERS

Lesson 1
Roles in Relationships

I believe that one of the most challenging areas in life is relationships. Each person speaks a different language out of their own experience, perspective and personal style. We have all experienced the frustration that results from misinterpretation and misunderstanding. As difficult as it may seem, we must learn to communicate with others in a healthy manner. The Bible has a lot to say about how we are to communicate with one another; how husbands and wives are to treat one another; how we are to raise our children; how employers and employees are to get along and how to treat our neighbor in general. Our relationship with God is central and all other relationships flow from it.

We will start with the roles and responsibilities of husbands and wives.

Husband/wife relationships
The marriage relationship was initiated by God in the Garden of Eden and is honorable in His sight. The Lord said that it was not good for man to live alone and so He created a suitable help meet to complete him.

Read Genesis 2:18-25. What three principles do you see in this passage?

____

____

____

____

We see the principles of **leaving, cleaving** and **weaving**. A man and his wife are no longer under the authority of their parents; once they are married, their primary human relationship is their mate. Cleaving speaks of being welded together; the marriage relationship must be based on commitment, not feelings (feelings can change). God holds us accountable to our vows (commitment, promise) for a lifetime. Determine in your heart that divorce (or the talk of separation, quitting, "throwing in the towel") is not an option. Weaving speaks of the combining of lives; husbands and wives are to function as a team. They are to share their hopes, dreams and goals. "...your personal responsibilities are more important than your "rights"....the teaching of rights breeds rebellion. The teaching of responsibilities brings revival. Many couples spend a lifetime fixated on their rights and they set out to make their mate meet their demands. They learn to see their mate as the major problem in the marriage and set out to change them. They fail to see their own responsibility, let alone work on fulfilling it."[1]

There is a lot more to the marriage relationship than we realize. God designed it to be a picture of the relationship between Christ and His church (the global church; all Christ followers). Let's see what we can learn from Christ's relationship with His bride, the church that we can apply to the roles of a husband and a wife.

Read Ephesians 5:22-33; I Peter 3:1-9.

List the characteristics of the husband:

____

____

____

List the responsibilities of the wife:

____

____

____

[1] Jim Binney, *The Ministry of Marriage*, Introduction, p. xiii.

Just as Christ is the head of His church, so the husband is the head of the home (responsible, initiator, provider). God calls him to **love** (care for and value) his wife as his own body and to sacrifice on her behalf as Christ gave up His life for His church. He is to **understand** her (be a learner) and to live in understanding with her. He is also commanded to **treat her as fragile** (Proverbs 18:22) and to be her **protector** (physically, emotionally and spiritually). Notice he is to rule with love and not as a dictator. Jesus washed His disciples' feet in order to teach us to be humble and to live a life of a servant; **a true leader is a servant that leads by example.** (John 13:14-15)

The responsibility of the wife is to **respect** and **be subject to** her husband as the church is to be subject to Her Lord. She is a fitting helper (Genesis 2:18); a companion, completing her husband in every way (physically, emotionally, spiritually, intellectually, parentally). A wise woman realizes that her husband's greatest need is for respect. He needs to be esteemed, admired and honored. This in no way makes her inferior to him. When she shows him respect (versus criticism, nagging or belittling), he will naturally respond with the love she most desires.[2]

There are also mutual responsibilities expected of all believers that may be applied to the marriage relationship. Read Ephesians 4:26, 29-30, 32; 5:21; I Peter 3:8-9; Philippians 2:3-4; list them below.

____

____

____

____

We are to be subject to one another, kind, tender-hearted, looking out for the needs of others and not just our own, forgiving one another. We are to speak (no silent treatment) the truth (honesty) lovingly with words that edify and not tear down (attack the problem, not the person). We are to maintain unity and avoid carrying grudges (stay current) by resolving conflicts as they occur (otherwise we open ourselves up to resentment, hatred, more conflict and distortion of future problems).

---

[2] Emerson Eggeridge, *Love and Respect*, Chapters 1-2.

Sinful men and women make a mess out of what God designed to be a wonderful relationship. Out of selfishness and pride they hurt each other deeply. I Peter 3:8-9 sums it up; be good to each other, kindhearted.

Many Christians seem to get their notions of love from the Love Boat instead of the Love Book. They get their ideas of marriage from the romance novels instead of the Bible and their notions of sex from the Playboy philosophy instead of the pages of Scripture. In all probability you have borrowed from some of these sources in forming your own views about marriage. It is the challenge of believers everywhere, and especially Christian partners of the marriage union, to refuse to conform to the thinking of the world and replace worldly philosophies with biblical theology.[3]

Parent/child relationships

Children

Read Ephesians 6:1-3. What is the command to children?

____

____

____

Children have a two-fold responsibility toward their parents; they are to **obey** and to **honor** (notice the two are interchangeable). Interestingly, this command comes with a promise (blessing always follows obedience). What is the promise?

____

____

____

[3] Jim Binney, *the Ministry of Marriage*, Introduction, p. xii.

Parents

What goals do you have for your children? What kind of individuals do you want them to grow up to be? What are your hopes and dreams for them? Are these goals and dreams related to their spiritual well-being?

The goal of parenting is to prepare our children to leave the home nest and fly successfully for themselves by thinking and acting biblically regarding life and the issues of life.[4]

I probably speak for many Christian parents when I say that my goals and expectations for my children are to know and walk with God, to be content/ fulfilled, well-adjusted individuals that possess good character (honesty, integrity, hardworking), emotionally and financially independent. Our children are created in the image (moral character) of God and entrusted to our care for a short time before they are out on their own. The task is an awesome one! God's Word does not leave us without guidance.

Today, many Christians carry excess and unnecessary baggage on their journey with Christ due to poor self-esteem developed while they were children. As parents, it is imperative that we raise our children to know Christ and to have healthy, balanced perspectives of who they are: sinful, but redeemed (bought), highly valued and loved by God.
To communicate acceptance and self-esteem:

First, know your child. Know his or her true abilities and interests. Each child should be uniquely considered, apart from siblings. Second, clearly verbalize your expectations. Third, praise your children for genuine effort. Warm praise and respect will encourage the growth of positive self-esteem.[5]

Read Ephesians 6:4 and summarize below.

____

____

____

[4] NANC - *Biblical Parenting for the 21st Century.*

[5] Dennis and Barbara Rainey, *Moments Together for Couples.*

The Father is commanded not to incite his children to a lifestyle of anger (open rebellion or passive hostility) but to nourish and train them in the ways of the Lord. This training implies instruction as well as discipline and correction. This is done by establishing, explaining and then enforcing appropriate rules and boundaries. We enforce rules by modeling (I Thess. 1:5-6), training (I Timothy 4:7-8), motivating (I Thess. 2:11-12) and chastising (Hebrews 12:5-12). It is our responsibility to teach them to establish their own convictions about God and His Word and the issues of life (priorities, work, relationships, money, etc).[6]

It is very important for parents to keep the communication lines open with their children (the love and acceptance has been laid down as a foundation) so when the time comes to teach, they will be more likely to listen to our instruction.

Employer/employee relationships

Read Ephesians 6:5-9. Paul is addressing slaves and instructing them to work hard for their masters, especially if their masters are unbelievers. We can apply this to our jobs and our relationships with our employers (as our culture has changed and we no longer own slaves; thankfully, every man and woman is free in Christ and has equal standing before God - read Galatians 3:28, Romans 2:11).

What are Paul's instructions to slaves? (Ephesians 6: 5-8)

____

____

What are Paul's instructions to masters? (Ephesians 6:9)

____

____

---

[6] NANC.

Employees are to be subject to their employers with sincerity; they are to work hard as if they are working for the Lord. It is freeing to know that we are working for the Lord and that He is the One that will reward us. Often the work place is not equitable and we may not get the recognition and encouragement for a job well done. We can take heart that our hard work is seen by God and that He will be the One to reward us.

Employers are told not to show partiality and to remember that they too answer to the Lord. This is a good reminder of who is ultimately in charge. With this reminder, employers should treat their employees with kindness and fairness.

God provides work as a way for us to meet our own needs. What is your view of work?

____

____

____

Where are your priorities? Do you work to live or live to work? Think about it! What are you trying to gain? Do you use the resources God has given you to help others? Do you give to see God's work advance? Or are you accumulating in order to use only on yourself?

What changes (thinking or behavior) do you need to make? Write your thoughts below.

____

____

____

____

Neighbor

Read Mark 12:30-31. What does Jesus command?

____

____

____

Who is your neighbor?

____

____

____

According to Jesus, the two greatest commandments are to love the Lord with all your heart, soul, mind and strength and to love your neighbor as yourself. Our neighbor is anyone we rub shoulders with. No one hates themselves; by nature we are selfish and want the best for ourselves. The golden rule teaches us to treat others like we want to be treated. (Matthew 7:12) Picture our work place, our neighborhoods, our communities and our society if everyone loved and treated one another as they themselves want to be treated. It's refreshing to meet people that are gracious and kind; be that person!

Challenge: Make a conscious effort to put this into practice for one full day. Write your experience below. What did you learn?

____

____

____

To recap everything we studied in this lesson.

Wives	**RESPECT**	Be subject to husband as to the Lord; gentle, chaste, values the adornment of the heart more than outer appearance; picture of the church subject to Christ
Husbands	**LOVE**	Selfless, sacrificing, servant, nourish, cherish, honor and live in understanding with his wife; responsible for her spiritual welfare; picture of Christ as the head of the church
Children	**OBEY & HONOR**	It will be well with you and live long = blessing
Parents	**DO NOT PROVOKE TO ANGER; TRAIN & INSTRUCT IN THE LORD**	Nurture, train, correct, pass down the faith; help children develop their own convictions
Employer	**DO NOT THREATEN (intimidate); DO NOT SHOW PARTIALITY**	Remembering God is the ultimate master
Employee	**OBEY & RESPECT**	Respect their employer's position, be genuine, hardworking, focused, obey them as to the Lord (good work ethic)
Neighbor	**LOVE AS YOURSELF**	Treat others as you want to be treated

A repeated theme in every relationship is that we are to behave as unto to the Lord; to love, respect and submit to earthly authorities as unto the

Lord. **It starts with submitting to Christ's authority in our own lives and then, submitting to earthly authorities that He has placed over us.** This is not easy, but *"I can do all things through Christ who strengthens me."* (Philippians 4:13)

Is there a relationship in your life that needs to change (realigned according to what you learned)?

____

____

How can you apply these principles to this relationship?

____

____

____

____

____

____

____

____

Lesson 2
The Body of Christ

When we accept Christ as Savior we not only enter into a wonderful relationship with Him, but we become part of the family of God. We become part of what the Bible refers to as the Body of Christ. Believers from all around the world make up the Body, and in turn become brothers and sisters in Christ. As I have traveled to different countries, I've been privileged to meet other Christians. They may look different and speak a different language and come from a different culture, but we experience this amazing connection. This connection is because we have the same Savior and the same Spirit living within us. This incredible bond is real because we live by the same biblical principles and share the same values and goals. In other words, we are traveling the same spiritual path.

I Corinthians 12:12-13
For as the body is _____ and has many members, but all the members of that one body, being many, are _____ body, so also is Christ. For by _____ Spirit we were all baptized into _____ body—whether Jews or Greeks, whether slaves or free—and have all been made to drink into _____ Spirit.

Believers from every walk of life (different nationalities, different economic and educational status, etc.) are **one** in Christ. As with any family, members have responsibilities toward one another. Look up the following references and note these responsibilities in the space below.

Galatians 5:13, 15

____

____

Ephesians 4: 2, 25, 32; 5:21

____

____

Philippians 1:27; 2:2-3

____

____

Colossians 3:9, 13, 16

____

____

I Thessalonians 5:11

____

____

Hebrews 10:24

____

____

James 5:16

____

I Peter 4:10

These are but a few of the *"one another"* verses mentioned in the New Testament. As part of the Body of Christ, we must take our responsibilities toward one another seriously because God commands it. We need to love, serve and encourage each other. We need to pray, forgive, speak the truth, bear one another's burdens and stimulate each other to love and good works. Read through the above list again; notice some are do's and some are don'ts.

Take time to think about how you can apply these things in your relationship with other Christians in your church, Sunday school class, co-workers, friends, etc. Write your thoughts (be specific – who do you need to forgive, how can you encourage, etc).

Our focus is on our brother/sister in the Lord and for their good. Our motive is to see them built up in the faith and this is done out of a heart of love and gratitude for everything God has done for us. **This will build great unity and strength within the Body of believers and will bring much honor to God.**

The Ten Commandments were given to the children of Israel as guidelines for life and relationships. Let's spend some time looking at them. Read Exodus 20:1-17 and list the Ten Commandments. Think about how to apply them to your life; write down your thoughts.

Commandment One:
"I am the LORD your God...you shall have no other gods before Me." What is your #1 priority? What do you spend most of your time thinking about and doing?

____

____

Commandment Two:
"You shall not make for yourself a carved image" (anything you put before God is an idol)

____

____

Commandment Three:
"You shall not take the name of the LORD your God in vain, for the LORD will not hold him guiltless who takes His name in vain." How often do we casually say "oh my God" or "Jesus"?

____

____

Commandment Four:
"Remember the Sabbath day, to keep it holy" Do you go to church on Sundays; work, shop and do a lot of busy work on Sunday instead of resting and making it God's day?

Commandment Five:
"Honor your father and your mother, that your days may be long upon the land which the LORD your God is giving you." Do you honor your parents? (Adult children still need to show respect.)

Commandment Six:
"You shall not murder." (To have hate in your heart is to be like a murderer)

Commandment Seven:
"You shall not commit adultery." (To lust or fantasize is the same as committing adultery)

Commandment Eight:
"You shall not steal." Are you completely honest in all your dealings?

Commandment Nine:
"You shall not bear false witness against your neighbor." Do you gossip or criticize?

Commandment Ten:
"You shall not covet your neighbor's house; you shall not covet your neighbor's wife, nor his male servant, nor his female servant, nor his ox, nor his donkey, nor anything that is your neighbor's." Are you jealous or envious of anyone; do you rejoice over others' misfortune?

Aren't you thankful that we do not live under the law? We have all broken every one of God's commandments. Thanks be to God for His Son Jesus Christ who forgives our sins and extends to us grace (unmerited favor). We too must extend the same grace to our brothers and sisters. We can do that by giving them the benefit of the doubt, by not being easily offended, by letting offenses roll off our backs and by remembering how much God forgives us.

What about the flip side; how about being proactive and being a blessing to one another? Gary Smalley and John Trent in their book "The Blessing" discuss the wonderful old tradition from the time of Abraham, Isaac and Jacob. This remarkable book shows "how to be a blessing and how to pass that life-changing blessing on to your parents, spouse, children and friends."[7] Smalley and Trent detail the five elements of giving a blessing: meaningful touch, the spoken word, the expression of high value, the description of a special future and the application of genuine commitment. They devote one chapter to our call as the church to be a blessing to others; God designed the church to be a caring community.

---

[7] Gary Smalley & John Trent, Ph.D., The Blessing, pp. 24; 185-195.

This is what it can look like: "with one young lady who had broken an engagement, providing the blessing meant simply taking her hands and crying with her. For a man, it involved a brother in Christ picturing a special future for him that gave him the confidence to tackle a difficult new assignment. Still another woman needed to know she was of high value to her friend and to the Lord after a week of listening to her employer say she was worthless.[8]

Summarize I Corinthians 12:26.

____

____

Is there someone you can bless today? Ask God how you can be a blessing to him/her?

____

____

____

____

We looked at the Old Testament and the Ten Commandment, now we will look at what the New Testament teaches about relationships. Read and record your insights. John 13:35; 15:12; Romans 12:10.

____

____

____

____

[8] Ibid, p. 191.

Friendships are among the most valuable things in life. They take a commitment of time and energy. There needs to be transparency, accountability, expressions of affirmation and thanks. Repairing a troubled friendship requires humility to admit our faults as well as effort and time to fix the problem. Perhaps it resulted from a misunderstanding, an unresolved conflict, or one person's busyness. After recognizing the problem, apologize for your part in it without justifying wrong actions or blaming others.[9]

Part of our responsibility within the Body of Christ is to resolve conflicts quickly and not allow them to fester. Let's look at the biblical way to deal with conflict. Read Matthew 18:15-17.

How should we handle conflict?

____

____

____

What should be our motive?

____

____

____

The point here is to handle conflicts **directly** with the person involved and in **private**. We often talk to everyone but the person that has offended us; this is a huge mistake. Most things can be resolved when the people involved spend time discussing the situation and are earnestly trying to work things out. When a resolution cannot be reached, it is recommended that you take one other person with you that perhaps would help mediate or act as a witness (an impartial person). It is important to note that the motive for the private and direct confrontation is to win your brother;

[9] Charles Stanley, *In Touch Daily Devotionals*, Building Solid Friendships and Saving Troubled Friendship, *www.intouch.org*.

that is the ultimate goal.

How have you handled conflict in the past?

____

____

____

What was the result?

____

____

____

How could it have been different had you applied this principle?

____

____

____

Read Ephesians 4:2-3; I Peter 3:8-9; 4:8. How can you apply these principles to your relationships now (be specific)?

____

____

____

Jesus put a high premium on love (especially within the Body). He claimed that it was proof that identifies believers as His followers. When Christians bicker and back bite, churches split and scandals of impropriety occur (in individual lives as well as corporately), there is a backlash of shame and disgrace to the church and to the name of Christ. How important it is to let love cover the multitude of sins rather than returning evil for evil; taking the higher road of forgiveness is truly the honorable way - it is God's way!

Read Ephesians 4:1-6. Find the key words in this passage:

____

____

____

Obviously love and unity are key in this passage; there is also the word **"one"** that is repeated. Believers are also united under one body, one Spirit, one hope, one Lord, one faith, one baptism, one God and Father. The world is watching; how do we as Christians conduct ourselves? Our relationships speak loudly to those around us. Are we showing them Christ-like behavior? How do you get along with other believers? How do you handle conflicts? Do you take God's principles seriously? Do you practice them in your relationships within the Body of Christ? If not, what changes do you need to make (in attitude or behavior)?

____

____

____

Can you imagine the world we would live in if people operated by the principle that says, "Don't look out for your own needs and interests, but for the needs of others?" Yet we live in a culture that tells us to forget about others and to look out for "Number One." What a terrible, dead-end philosophy that is!

One thing we should bear in mind about God's love is that it is patient. And as part of the body of Christ, our love should be patient as well.

Love is long-tempered.

A verse that would be good to think about today is 1 Corinthians 13:4, which says, "Love endures long."

Another way to translate that phrase is, "Love is long-tempered." This common New Testament term is used almost exclusively in speaking of being patient with people, rather than being patient with circumstances or events.

Love's patience is the ability to be inconvenienced again and again.

The last words of Stephen, the first martyr of the church, were those of patient forgiveness: "Lord, do not charge them with this sin" (Acts 7:60 NKJV). As he was dying, he prayed for his murderers rather than for himself. This is the same kind of love Jesus spoke of that turns the other cheek. It's the kind of love that has as its primary concern not its own welfare, but in the welfare of others.

Love is kind too.

And love is kind. Just as patience will take anything from others, kindness will give anything to others. To be kind means to be useful, serving, and gracious. It is active goodwill. Love not only feels generous; it is generous. Love not only desires the welfare of others; love works for it.

If, however, you wait for this emotion to come and settle over you like the morning dew, you may be waiting a long, long time. Remember, love is active. Love is kind. So just be kind, even if you don't feel kind. Step out with kind, loving actions, and your

> feelings will follow along behind.
>
> So carve out the time. Write the checks. Carry another's load. Invest yourself in really listening and lend a hand whether you feel competent or not. And most of all, be quick to forgive...as the Lord is quick to forgive you.[10]

In this lesson we had an opportunity to study what the Law (the Ten Commandments) teaches us. We saw our inability to follow the Law completely. The Law was given to us as a perfect standard of God; it shows us how far we fall short. We also studied our responsibilities to one another within the Body of Christ and how grace (what is not deserved) is extended. When we are insulted, our natural reaction is to insult or retaliate but God is calling us to extend grace, tolerance and patience, which is opposite to our natural response. Part of grace is to resolve conflicts in a godly way. We learned that the best way to resolve conflicts is the private and direct approach.

---

[10] Pastor Greg Laurie, Daily Devotion, Harvest Ministries, June 2, 2012.

SACRIFICE:

HOW SHOULD I SERVE WITH MY TIME, TALENTS AND RESOURCES

Lesson 3
Money, Riches, Tithing & Stewardship

There are two extreme views about money and riches. One view is that money brings happiness and the more we get, the happier we will be; our goal in life is to acquire as much as possible. We may become workaholics, marry into wealth, or steal it; we do whatever it takes. The other extreme is to think that money and riches are evil and that nothing good can come of having wealth. Both are far from the truth. Money in the right hands can bring about a lot of good (and joy to others); more ministries and churches can be funded, more missionaries can be sent to the field, and more people in need can be helped. A generous heart is a happy one. It's when money is hoarded or used only to satisfy our selfish desires that we discover how truly miserable we can be.

The Bible speaks to our hearts and our attitudes about money (whether we have money or not). What does money mean to you? How high is it on your priority list? We can be poor and yet money can be our god. The opposite is also true; we can be wealthy but money may not have a hold on us! Do you control your money or does it control you?

In this lesson, we will look at what the Bible says about money and the proper way to view it; we will also look at giving and stewardship.

Money and Riches

I Timothy 6:17-19
Command those who are rich in this present age not to be _______, nor to ______ in uncertain riches but in the living God, who ________ us richly all things to enjoy. Let them do _______, that they be rich in _______ works, ready to give, willing to _______ storing up for themselves a _______ foundation for the time to come, that they may lay hold on ____________ ________.

What does it say about riches?

____

What is the contrast?

____

According to verse 18, what are we to be rich in?

____

What are we to be ready to do?

____

Timothy is saying that riches are uncertain and not to depend on them but rather focus on God who will supply all our needs. He is teaching that it is more important to be rich in good works and ready to share with others.

Read James 2:1-7. What does this passage warn against?

____

What did you learn about money and wealth?

____

____

____

____

James is talking here about the sin of showing partiality. It is wrong to treat people based on their financial means. Riches do not make the person. We are to treat everyone with respect regardless of his/her financial status. We should hold all people in high esteem: from the janitor to the president. God shows no partiality; He is not a respecter of person (James 2); neither should we.

God is more concerned with our attitude about money. It is not money that is the root of all evil but the love of money. (I Timothy 6:10) Godliness with contentment is great gain. (I Timothy 6:6) What we do with our money says a lot about us. Jesus had much to say on this subject.

What is the warning in I John 2:15-17?

____

____

How does loving the world relate to money?

____

____

____

How should we view money and where should our focus be according to verse 17?

____

____

____

According to Matthew 6:21, 24 whatever is important to you is what your heart will cling to (your thoughts, desires, priorities). Money can divide our allegiance and it can stand in the way of serving God. How important is money to you; how tightly do you hold on to it, what do you do with it? Think about what you spend your money on; this will shed light on what is most important to you (family, material possessions, entertainment, hobbies). Write your thoughts.

____

____

____

____

____

____

____

When we hold money in high importance, we become a slave to it, and whatever we are a slave to becomes our god. Another way to put it is, whatever you are most preoccupied with is where your heart is, and where your heart is indicates your master! There is only room in our heart for one master; our allegiance will be to either money or God. (Matthew 6:24) Do you need to make any changes in this area (attitude or behavior)?

____

____

____

____

Have you ever felt that having more money would solve your problems? If only I had this or that, I would be satisfied? A few years ago there was a Pennsylvania lottery winner who went home with $16.2 million. He later said that his life has been a total nightmare and he wished it had never happened.

There was a study done on happiness where the USA ranked 15 while countries like Colombia, Costa Rica and Mexico ranked in the top 5. What does this say when the wealthiest country in the world ranks so low on the happiness scale? Possessions and riches won't make us happy or satisfied. Look at the lives of celebrities. If riches could bring happiness why are so many turning to drugs, alcohol and even taking their own lives.

Giving

Read I Corinthians 3:9-15. How are believers described? (vs. 9)

____

____

What is the foundation being laid down? (vs. 9-11)

____

____

What are the two foundations and what do they represent? (vs. 12)

____

____

How will the foundation be tested? (vs. 14-15)

____

What is this passage teaching?

How does this relate to giving?

Keep in mind that Paul has been writing about wisdom in the first three chapters of I Corinthians. The Corinthians were trying to build their church by man's wisdom, the wisdom of this world, when they should have been depending on the wisdom of God as found in the Word. *When we dig deep in the Word of God, we will mine gold, silver, and jewels and build these truths into our lives.*[11] The Book of Proverbs presents the wisdom of the Word of God as a treasure to be sought, protected, and invested in daily life (Suggested reading: 3:13-15a; 2:1-5; 8:10-11).

At the end of our life, when we stand before God, all of our work, our giving, our motives as well as our actions, will be judged by fire. Those things done for God will be as gold, silver and precious stones and will remain, but all other things will be burned away like wood, hay and stubble. **Our life and our life's work is the foundation; our foundation must be Jesus Christ.** This passage causes us to evaluate what we are doing with our life; are we living and working with the priority of eternal things or temporal things? If we invest our time and resources in things that are eternal, we will have an eternal reward. It will be a sad day for many that invested their lives in

[11] John MacArthur, *The MacArthur New Testament Commentary*, Matthew 24-28, p. 341.

temporal things; they will see those things go up in smoke. What a clear warning to us now! Don't spend precious time and resources on things that will not last. Use your time on earth wisely; redeem the time. Our goal as His children is to one day stand in His presence unashamed and to hear the words *"well done, good and faithful servant"*. (Matthew 25:23) Jesus said that the person who listens to His words and obeys them is likened to a man who built his house on a rock; when the winds and storms came, the house remained standing but the person who does not obey, he is like a man who built his house on sand; when the winds and storms came, the house fell. (Matthew 7:24-27)

Read Luke 12:13-2.1 Where was the rich man's focus?

____

____

What did Jesus call the rich man? Why?

____

____

What was missing in the life of the rich man (hint: his focus will give you a clue)

____

____

What is this passage teaching about riches and wealth?

____

____

Notice the rich man was rich in material possessions but his life was void of God; he lacked an eternal perspective. His focus was limited to this life and what will bring him happiness. Jesus called him a fool. That's a strong word that describes one that lacks wisdom. When it comes to wealth, human nature always wants more. One of the wealthiest men in the world was asked when will he have enough, and his answer was 'a little bit more' (vs. 18 tear down and build larger). A self-centered life of possessions and pleasures will not bring happiness. In fact the more we focus on ourselves the more miserable we become; focusing on others brings a sense of joy and freedom.

Covetousness is an unquenchable thirst for getting more and more of something we think we need in order to be truly satisfied. It may be a thirst for money or what money can buy, or even a thirst for position and power. Mark Twain once defined "civilization" as "a limitless multiplication of unnecessary necessities," and he was right. In fact, many Christians are infected with covetous-ness and do not know it. They think that Paul's admonition in I Timothy 6 applies only to the "rich and famous." Measured by the living standards of the rest of the world, most believers in America are indeed wealthy people.[12] It is hard to imagine, but two thirds of the world lives in poverty.

How do you view money? Do you view money differently after reading these verses?

____

____

____

Meditate on I Corinthians 3:1. What foundation are you building on? Take a minute to consider this and write down your thoughts.

____

____

[12] Ibid, p. 220.

Whether you have a little or a lot is not the question. Make a commitment right now to dedicate your money to God and ask Him to help you keep it in the proper perspective.

Let's put what we have learned in perspective of what God teaches in His Word.

Extremes	
Money is evil vs. Money is everything	Be rich in good works
Too tight vs. Overspending	
Hoarding vs. Debt	Share with others
Controlled/mastered by money vs. Out of control/irresponsible with money	God desires that we have a healthy balance
Misuses of money	
Love of money - possessions, pleasures, power, notoriety, security	Trust God to supply our needs
Use money as a means to control or influence	Giving, helping others
Showing partiality	God is not a respecter of person; Be impartial
Foundation	
Wood, hay, stubble (TEMPORAL)	Gold, silver & precious stones (ETERNAL)
Building on sand, fall, great loss	Building on rock, stand
Desiring more - Covetousness	Godliness with Contentment
Rich in possessions	Rich in God
Focus on this life	There is more than this life
Fool	Wise

If this expresses the desire of your heart, commit it now in prayer.

Father, I recognize that everything I have is from you, and I want to commit my money and wealth to you. Help me to keep my possessions in the proper perspective. I want to honor you with my money and possessions and serve only you as my master and Lord. In Jesus name, Amen.

Tithing

Giving to the local church or funding a Christian ministry is referred to as tithing. The Old and New Testament teaches important truths on this subject. As we covered in the previous section, money in itself is not evil but it is the love of money that brings about evil. We stressed several things; God is more concerned with our attitude; what we do with our money says a lot about us; we tend to spend our money on things we value!

Read the following passages and write down what you learn about giving.

I Corinthians 16:1-2

____

____

II Corinthians 9:6

____

____

II Corinthians 9:7

____

____

Mark 12:41-44

Malachi 3:10

Our giving or tithing is to reflect a **grateful heart**. It is to be as an act of **worship**. We are to give **cheerfully** and **generously**; we are to give to **further the work of God**. Many think they need to give 10% of their income but the New Testament teaches that we are to give in proportion to what God gives us. It has been said 'you can't outgive God'. Those who give bountifully receive bountifully from God. Matthew 6:33 teaches that when we put God first, He will take care of everything else. The widow in Mark 12:41-44 gave sacrificially while others with wealth gave out of their surplus. Jesus concluded that in God's economy, the widow gave more than the others!

What is your attitude about giving? Is it a priority?

How do you give?

Do you give generously, sacrificially or only after all the bills have been paid then you consider giving?

____

____

____

Make giving to God a priority and watch how He provides for all your needs. He is faithful to take care of you and to bless your finances.

Let's look at why it is important to give **cheerfully**, **generously** and **proportionately**. Read Matthew 6:19-24. What is Jesus teaching about giving?

____

____

____

____

This life is not all there is! Christians have a different perspective on life and they also have different priorities than non-believers. We can store wealth here on earth, but it can be destroyed or stolen; Jesus is teaching that it is more worthwhile to invest our wealth in eternal things. When we give our tithes to God, we are in essence sending it on ahead.

Pastor Greg Laurie tells of a farmer, known for his frugality, who owned a cow that gave birth to two calves. He said to his wife, "I am going to dedicate one of these calves to the Lord." Knowing his miserly ways, she was very surprised and asked which one he was planning to give to the Lord. "I haven't decided yet, but I'll let you know," he said. A few days went by, and again she asked which calf he was giving to the Lord. "I'm still thinking about it," he told her. Then one day, one of the calves got sick. It grew worse and worse, until one night the farmer walked up on the porch with the calf draped over his arms. He said to his wife, "Honey, I have bad news. The Lord's calf just died."[13]

Many times, we tend to give God what we don't really want ourselves. If God is important, then why do we give Him our leftovers? We see in Malachi 1:7-8 that God does not want our leftovers. *"You offer defiled food on My altar, But say,' In what way have we defiled You?' By saying, 'The table of the LORD is contemptible.' And when you offer the blind as a sacrifice, Is it not evil? And when you offer the lame and sick, Is it not evil? Offer it then to your governor! Would he be pleased with you? Would he accept you favorably?" Says the LORD of hosts."* God gave us His best. Let's give Him ours.

Stewardship

Read Matthew 25:14-30. Summarize this parable (assignment, characters, outcome, etc.)

____

____

____

This parable is teaching principles regarding stewardship. The master addresses three of his servants and gives them a different amount of money (a talent was worth about twenty years of wages) according to their abilities. The talents represent opportunities to use their abilities, while the master determines those abilities. The servants were to take the talents and put them to work for the master just as every believer must seize every opportunity to use their abilities for Christ. This parable is measuring the faithfulness of the servants to use what their master has given them. The faithful servants used their talents wisely and were then promoted to rulers; for their efforts, they were ushered into their joy. The last servant decided to do nothing with what his master had given him. Now is the time for us to work and to toil and to be faithful with the opportunities God gives us.

---

[13] Greg Laurie, *Daily Devotions*, Harvest Ministries, 2008, www.harvest.org.

The time for rewards and rest will come one day when our Lord and Master returns.

Take a minute and examine your life. What do you spend your time and money on? Are they things that will last for eternity or are they temporary and self-indulgent? Write down your thoughts.

What talents and abilities did God entrust to you? What opportunities do you have at home, school or work? Are you making the most of those opportunities to serve others, and to serve Christ? Are you being a good example and a witness to others?

In what ways have you done well?

In what ways do you need to improve?

There are many ways that we can give to God. We can give to the church that is doing God's work and proclaiming His Word so people can come to a relationship with God. We can give to a person in need. We can also give of ourselves in service to others. Whatever the opportunity, give out of a heart of love and gratitude for the One who sent His only Son that you might have life everlasting; give to the One who paid a high price on the cross so you can have a relationship with Him.

Let's look at what the wise men gave to Jesus at His birth. Read Matthew 2:11. What gifts did they bring? What is the significance of these gifts?

They brought gold, myrrh and frankincense. Don't you think these are strange gifts to present to an infant? They were obviously symbolic of the life of Jesus Christ. The gold was a proper gift for a king; the frankincense was used by a high priest when entering the temple to present the people to God; the myrrh (for embalming) represented His death for the world.

What gifts can we give God? Think about it, what does God want us to give to Him?

____

____

____

____

God wants us to give Him our lives. He wants us to give Him our hopes, dreams, talents, abilities and our future. He wants us to come with no strings attached and say to Him 'Lord do with me as you wish'; 'I want what you want for my life'.

"Now we see things imperfectly as in a poor mirror, but then we will see everything with perfect clarity...." (1 Corinthians 13:12a) Oswald Chambers said, "Doubt is not always a sign that a man is wrong. It may be a sign that he is thinking." There is a difference between doubt and unbelief. Doubt is a matter of the mind. Unbelief is a matter of the heart. Doubt is when we cannot understand what God is doing and why He is doing it. Unbelief is when we refuse to believe God's Word and do what He tells us to do. We must not confuse the two. God will deal with your doubt through His Word. When you are facing doubt, that is not the time to close the Bible. That is the time to open it and let God speak to you. Maybe you have been doubting God's ways in your life. Maybe you have been asking "why" a lot lately. Maybe His timing doesn't seem to make any sense. The Bible says, *"All that I know now is partial and incomplete, but then I will know everything completely, just as God knows me now"* (1 Corinthians 13:12b). It all will be resolved in that final day when we stand before God. God doesn't ask us to understand everything. He asks us to trust Him and follow Him.[14]

---

[14] Greg Laurie, *Daily Devotions*, When we doubt, Harvest Ministries, 2008, www.harvest.org

We must remember that everything we have has been given to us by God and that we are to be good stewards (caretakers) of it (our time, our talents and our money). Your giving, or lack of, reflects what's important to you; it reflects your heart's condition.

In the Old Testament, God taught the children of Israel the concept of giving from their first fruits, also known as the Feast of Weeks or Pentecost. Read Leviticus 23:9-10 and Exodus 34:22. Record God's command.

____

____

____

For centuries Israel was an agricultural people depending for her sustenance on the produce of the land. Pentecost was the Feast of the Ingathering of the firstfruits of the wheat harvest, a thanksgiving festival in which Israel expressed her dependence on God for harvest and daily bread. The Feast of Weeks was a most popular holiday, falling in early summer...[15]

The children of Israel were to give of the first fruits which would show their faith in God to provide the rest of the harvest. God is teaching a very important principle here about giving. We are putting God first when we tithe from the top, from our first fruits and not from the leftovers. The significance is that we are saying 'God, I will give to you first and will trust you to provide for the rest'. What is your attitude towards tithing? Do you give right off the top? How do you think God wants you to give?

____

____

____

Look at what God will do for you as you obey Him and make Him your priority. Read Deut. 28:1-8; Ezekiel 34:25-31. In the space below write out

[15] Victor Buksbazen, *The Gospel in The Feasts of Israel*, p. 15.

Malachi 3:10.

Giving of your first fruits is an act of faith. Are you trusting God to provide for all your needs? Put Him first and let Him provide for the rest. What changes do you need to make (in attitude or behavior)?

Lesson 4
Spiritual Gifts

God gives every believer a package of spiritual gifts with the purpose of serving Him and serving others in the Body of Christ. Jesus *"set aside the privileges of deity and took on the status of a slave, became human! It was an incredibly humbling process. He didn't claim special privileges. Instead, he lived a selfless, obedient life and then died a selfless, obedient death - and the worst kind of death at that: a crucifixion"* (Philippians. 2:7--8 MSG). Let's follow his example. Let's *"put on the apron of humility, to serve one another"* (1 Peter 5:5 TEV). Jesus entered the world to serve. We can enter our jobs, our homes, our churches. Servanthood requires no unique skill or seminary degree. Regardless of your strengths, training, or church tenure, you can love the overlooked, swallow your pride (and your own agenda) and serve. *"Throw yourselves into the work of the Master, confident that nothing you do for him is a waste of time or effort"* (1 Corinthians. 15:58 MSG).[16]

In this lesson we will look at what the Bible calls spiritual gifts, their purpose and how to use them. There is a spiritual gifts inventory in the Appendix that will give you the opportunity to discover your own spiritual gifts and how you can use them as you serve Christ in your local church.

What is the purpose of spiritual gifts?

I Corinthians 12:7; I Peter 4:10

____

____

Ephesians 4:12

____

---

[16] Max Lucado, *Upwords with Max Lucado*, Serve One Another, 2008.

____

Romans 1:11

____

____

Spiritual gifts are to manifest the Holy Spirit and are given to us for the common good; to be used to serve others and to build up the Body of Christ. They are to be used to make others strong and to help them use their own gifts in service. Theologically we can say that spiritual gifts work in the spiritual realm and natural talents in the natural realm. Since all Christians are human beings, they have natural talents as well as spiritual gifts. Since not all human beings are Christians, those who do not have the Holy Spirit cannot have spiritual gifts. Even a Christian might have a natural talent for public speaking but not necessarily have the gift of prophecy.[17] It is important to understand that spiritual gifts are supernaturally given to believers for ministry; they come as a result of salvation.

Spiritual gifts are different from talents and abilities. They are given by God to every believer to use for serving others and for building up the church. Spiritual gifts are given to strengthen the unity between believers, to strengthen our testimony before the world and to increase our effectiveness in service. God does not call the equipped, He equips the called. He equips believers with talents, abilities, spiritual gifts, time and resources. Interestingly, the word ministries in I Corinthians 12:5, is from the same basic Greek term as serve, servant and deacon (one who serves).[18] Jesus said about Himself, *"For even the Son of Man did not come to be served, but to serve, and to give His life a ransom for many."* (Mark 10:45)

God asks us to be faithful and unselfish with what He has given us; these gifts are not for our own self-gratification. We may exercise our talents, skills, intelligence, and other natural abilities in our own power, but only the Giver of spiritual gifts can empower them and make them effective. We must be pure from sin and be willing to be used, in order that the Holy Spirit can make our gifts productive. Both the bestowing and the empowering are the Lord's work.[19]

---

[17] Kenneth O. Gangel, *Unwrap Your Spiritual Gifts*, pp. 11-12

[18] John MacArthur, The MacArthur New Testament Commentary, 1 Corinthians, p. 291.

[19] Ibid, p. 292.

Read Matthew 16:24. What must happen first before we can serve God or live for Him?

____

____

____

Jesus said that we can't serve Him or live for Him without first dying to self. He said that we must first deny ourselves, take up our cross and follow Him. (Matthew 16:24) Taking up the cross speaks of dying to ourselves and wanting God's will more than our own. It does not mean that your life is ruined when you decide to walk with God. What it does mean is that you now will have life and have it more abundantly as Jesus promised because you want God's will more than your own. Jesus said, *"Whoever desires to save his life will lose it, but whoever loses his life for My sake and the gospel's will save it"* (Mark 8:35). Are you taking up the cross and following Jesus? Bearing the cross will affect and influence every aspect of your life. The result will be life as it was meant to be lived: in the perfect will of God.[20]

Read I Corinthians 12:13-31 and Galatians 3:28. How are we to use our spiritual gifts?

____

____

____

We are all one in Christ; regardless of race, gender or economic status. God arranged the parts of the body as He wished. (I Corinthians 12:13, 18) It is important to note that all parts (gifts) belong (15-16; 26), all are important (25), all are needed/necessary (21) and the ones that may seem less prominent, receive greater honor (22-24) so that there is no division or bias. These spiritual gifts (parts of the body) are for unity, to build up, to care for and to serve the Body of Christ (25-27).

---

[20] Greg Laurie, *Greg Laurie Daily Devotions, Cross Bearing*, 2008.

Now when we preach, teach, show mercy, help, lead, give or have faith, we find that our gift is a supernatural activity endowed and enabled by the Spirit of God. The gift manifests an attribute of Christ in order to build up the body. Thus Christ becomes real in the world. The gifts are not random, but they specifically find their source in God, their channel in the Spirit and their pattern, their example and their completeness in the person of Jesus Christ. They are essential because they manifest Christ and build up the church.[21] The Holy Spirit determines and allocates the gifts as He wills.

With that foundation, list the spiritual gifts mentioned in each passage.

Romans 12:6-8

____

____

I Corinthians 12:8-11

____

____

I Corinthians 12:28-30

____

____

Look at the list of gifts above. They can be grouped in three categories. What are they?

____

____

---

[21] John MacArthur, Jr., *Spiritual Gifts*, p. 24.

How does I Corinthians 12 end? Notice what the topic is in the following chapter: I Corinthians 13

____

____

____

We are not to seek certain gifts but the greater gifts are love, peace and joy. I Corinthians 13 reminds us that the greatest gift is love and that in anything we do we must do it with love otherwise it doesn't profit anything (useless or in vain).

There are three categories of spiritual gifts: Speaking, Serving and Supernatural

The speaking gifts include: prophecy, teaching, word of knowledge, word of wisdom, exhortation.

The serving gifts include: faith, helps, discernment of spirits, administration, serving, mercy, giving.

The supernatural gifts include: healing, miracles, speaking in tongues, interpretation of tongues.

The supernatural gifts, also referred to as temporary sign gifts were limited to the apostolic age and therefore ceased at that time. Their purpose was to authenticate the apostolic message as the Word of God, until the time when the Scriptures, His written Word, were completed and became self-authenticating.[22] Combining the teaching of the New Testament concerning "apostles" and "prophets" it appears that these men were special ministries given to the establishment of the church in its early ("foundation") stages, and that they were "confirming" the spoken word by the use of miraculous deeds, and giving special revelation to the early believers who only had the Old Testament to use and to understand. On the basis of this, there is no evidence that these two "gifts" are in operation today. With the completion of the New Testament, there would be no

---

[22] John MacArthur, *The MacArthur New Testament Commentary*, 1 Corinthians, pp. 297-298.

need for their continued ministry.[23]

What is the key (significant, repeated) word used in this passage and what does it reveal? I Corinthians 12:12-19

____

____

What else did you observe about the relationship between the members? vs.21-27

____

____

The key word is *"one"*; it is repeated 8 times in 8 verses. As believers, we are part of one body, one Spirit and one Lord. It is also significant because it shows us that we are both unified as well as diversified; one body but many members; one Spirit but many gifts. Notice how we are interdependent on one another and on the Lord, just as an eye cannot tell the hand that it is not needed within the body (21-27). Every person is needed; every gift is important and contributes to the work of the ministry. Also note that all the parts are equal (some are not more important than others) and necessary.

Read the list below and prayerfully consider your spiritual gifts in light of what you have learned.

- Your preferences and tendencies
- Your past Christian service experiences
- Your training or education (in the Word of God)
- Your evaluation of yourself against each gift (you will do this in the next section)

---

[23] David Hocking, *Spiritual Gifts, Their Necessity and use in the local church*, p. 11.

- Your degree of commitment to exercise your gift
- Area of service within the local church

Write your thoughts and ideas below.

____

____

____

____

____

Write out Philippians 3:14.

____

____

Let this be your goal, to press on for the prize. Be tenacious and never give up. Our prize is an incorruptible crown; our prize is to please our Lord and Savior and to bring Him honor and glory. What does it mean to bring Him glory? The word glory means to give the right value or proper worth. Christians are to showcase Christ to the world; we are His trophies!

In conclusion, *"no gift is the sign of superior spirituality or a higher level of walk with God. The key is not so much to seek new gifts as to recognize, develop and use the one(s) we have."*[24]

In the following section, you will answer a list of questions that will help you to evaluate your own package of spiritual gifts. Each gift is then defined in detail to give you a greater understanding. I hope you will approach this with great anticipation and an open heart.

---

[24] Kenneth O. Gangel, *Unwrap Your Spiritual Gifts*, p. 14.

Test & Evaluation

Go to the Appendix in the back and follow the instructions for the Spiritual Gifts Survey. Answer the questions and total your points in the boxes given then come back and bring your results to this page.

What are your three highest gifts?

God has called all of us to give, to intercede (pray) on behalf of others, to have faith, etc. Those who have those gifts seem to have a divine enablement; in other words a greater measure. Refer to the pages of definitions, characteristics and cautions for each gift. Get familiar with the different gifts and especially your top three.

Note your gifts with the lowest scores. Seek God in prayer and ask Him how He may want you to develop in these areas. Perhaps He is calling you to be more of an encourager, perhaps to step out on faith and trust Him for bigger things. Write out your thoughts below and talk to God about it.

Refer to the list of church ministries (in the Appendix). Look at the list and see if you can determine what gifts line up with these ministries (you do not need to do each one: this is simply an exercise to help you see how the different gifts can be used in the ministries of a local church) i.e. worship team = Creative Communication; funerals and special needs = Helps and Hospitality; treasurer and secretary = Administration, etc.

Look at your three highest gifts and ask God to show you where you can use your gifts. Name the ministry (or ministries) below. You may be very zealous to serve the Lord and others but I want to caution you against being over committed. The Lord taught us in Luke 14:28 to count the cost before jumping into anything. So be a wise steward and only commit to what you are able to faithfully accomplish without neglecting your walk with God or responsibilities to your family.

SPIRITUAL WARFARE:

WHO IS THE ENEMY AND HOW DO I OVERCOME

Lesson 5
The Flesh, The Devil, The World

Every believer quickly realizes that the Christian life is a battlefield. Our enemies are the **flesh**, the **devil** and the **world**. (Ephesians 2:1-3) The flesh is our old nature that is human and opposes God. The **devil** is referred to in the Bible by many names: Satan, Lucifer, accuser, adversary, murder, liar, tempter. The Devil's goal is to keep us from living for God and experiencing His power and His victory in our lives. The **world** is the culture or value system around us that opposes God and caters to the lusts of the flesh and the pride of life. (I John 2:15-17)

The good news is, Jesus Christ's death and resurrection overcame our enemies (John 16:33, Romans 6:1-6, Ephesians 1:19-23). We need to remember that the victory has already been won and that it is only by God's power that we fight these enemies. Keep in mind that this battle is not against human beings but against spiritual powers and we must in turn use spiritual weapons to defeat them (2 Corinthians 10:4-5; Ephesians 6:12). With all three of these enemies, the common denominator is sin. The bad news is as long as we live on this earth, we will have an internal as well as an external struggle with sin!

In this lesson, we will discuss the lust of the flesh and friendship with the world; in the next we will cover our struggle with the devil and the armor/ protection God provides us.

First, we will look at sin. In Psalm 32, David shows us that in order to understand forgiveness we must first understand sin. Write out Psalm 32:1-2.

____

____

____

Transgression (*pasha* in Hebrew) means rebel, transgress, revolt, a breach of relationship; those who reject God's authority. Sin (*hata* a in Hebrew) at its root is to miss a mark or way; a man is missing the goal or standard God has for him, is failing to observe the requirements of holy living. Iniquity (*awon* in Hebrew) at its root is guilt, punishment, to bend, to twist, or to deviate (both the deed and the consequences).

Let's first look at our struggle with the flesh. Remember, this is the old sinful nature that is in opposition with God. The Apostle Paul wrote about this; the old and new natures are always fighting for control. Read Romans 7:18-25. What did you learn about the two natures? Is there hope for us?

____

____

____

____

____

____

There is nothing good in our flesh. Paul paints a picture of the struggle against the flesh that goes on inside each of us. As born again believers, we desire to do what is right and to live for God, but our flesh is constantly fighting us for control. Praise God there is hope for us through the Lord Jesus Christ because of His victory on the cross over sin and death. Without Christ we are helpless against sin, but thankfully, Christ has broken the power of sin over us. Now when we sin it is because we choose to.

Read James 1:13-16. When are we tempted to sin? Where does the temptation begin?

____

____

Note the progress of events in verse 15. First, we are swept away by our lustful desires and then we commit the act. The Bible tells us that the wages of sin is death (which is spiritual separation from God). God is holy and our sin separates and breaks fellowship with Him. Sin leads to spiritual death.

Lust ↣ Sin ↣ Death

Can you relate?

Think of a time when you saw this played out in your life.

____

____

____

John 3:16 explains why God sent His Son.
For God so loved the world that He _____ His only begotten ______, that whoever _________ in Him should not perish but have ___________ __________. Jesus took the death sentence on Himself so we can have a connection/relationship with God.

One of the toughest battlegrounds is in the area of forgiving those who have hurt and offended us. This area is also used by the devil to destroy unity and keep us from experiencing freedom. We are commanded to forgive others as God has forgiven us and yet we struggle to let go of those offenses. How often are we to forgive according to Matthew 8:21-22?

____

____

Why are we to forgive? Matthew 18:23-35.

____

The illustration here is to show us that we are to forgive without limits and we are to forgive others because God has forgiven us a greater debt.

Let's look at what forgiveness is not

- excusing or condoning sin
- forgetting a person's sin. God has that power, but we do not. Forgiveness means that even though you remember the hurt, you give up the need to punish the other person
- denying your pain, hurt or anger. It may take time for your feelings to catch up and begin to fall in line with your decision to forgive
- stuffing your grief. There is genuine pain due to hurt. It may take time for the wound to heal, even though you forgive the person who offended you
- instant and full reconciliation. Even when you forgive, it can take time and effort by both parties to rebuild trust

Even at that moment, while suffering the most terrible abuse, *"Jesus said, Father, forgive them, for they do not know what they do."* (Luke 23:34) Note what our attitude should be; *"And be kind to one another, tenderhearted, forgiving one another, even as God in Christ forgave you."* (Ephesians 4:32)

This passage holds three lessons:

- Forgiveness embraces the offenders. Christ offered forgiveness to the very people who hurt Him the most. And that's not all-He offered it to them while they were still hurting Him.
- Forgiveness initiates. God desired your fellowship so much He took the initiative in forgiving you. He did not wait for you to earn it.
- Forgiveness gives up all rights to punish. God canceled your debt against Him. You deserve to die as the penalty for your sins. But God, knowing it was absolutely impossible for you to pay that debt, had Christ pay the penalty as a substitution for you.
- If you ever have trouble forgiving others, just remember what Christ did for you. And you didn't deserve it.[25]

Has someone ever hurt you or wronged you? Are you still holding it against them?

---

[25] Dennis and Barbara Rainey, *Moments Together for Couples, Forgiveness (Part 1 & 2).*

Is there someone (now or in your past) that you need to forgive (let it go)? How is extending forgiveness possible based on what you learned in this lesson?

What does forgiveness look like in this situation?

The culture we live in and this world's system is what is referred to in the Bible as the world. Keep in mind, this world is in direct opposition to God and His ways.

Read I John 2:15-17. What is the warning? What are the three elements mentioned as part of the world? Note verse 17. What will happen to the world and to its lusts? What is the contrast?

The warning is to not love the world and what the world has to offer.

John points out that the world system uses three devices to trap Christians: the lust (desire) of the flesh, the lust of the eyes, and the pride of life. These same devices trapped Eve back in the Garden: "And when the woman saw that the tree was good for food [the lust of the flesh], and that it was pleasant to the eyes [the lust of the eyes], and a tree to be desired to make one wise [the pride of life], she took of the fruit" (Genesis 3:6).[26]

The contrast is that the world and its lusts are passing away (will not last), but the person who follows God will live forever. The world appeals to us through our human desires, through what our eyes see (gateway to the mind) and through our sense of pride.

Let's look at James 4. Read the chapter and make a list of the pleasures of the flesh/world, how they manifest themselves (behavior) and the cure.

Pleasures	**The Evidence**	**The Cure**

Pleasures that appeal to the flesh/world can be: love, sex, power, fame, respect, control, prestige, possessions, talents. These worldly desires or friends of the world, manifest themselves as: quarreling (:1), envy (:2), selfishness (:3), wrong motive, unanswered prayer, fond of the world (:4), lack of commitment to God (:5), insensitive to the Holy Spirit (:5), judging others (:11-12), forgetting to include God (:13, 15), loss of eternal perspective

[26] Warren W. Wiershe, *The Bible Exposition Commentary*, p. 493

(:14), arrogance (:16), know what is right but not doing it (:17).

Friendship with the world (James 4:4)	**Worldly Believer**
Teaches independence from God	independent
Teaches opposition to God	separated
Teaches disobedience to God	rebellious
Distracts from God	fleshly
Deceives (promises answers to life)	self-sufficient
Drowns out God's voice	distracted
Gives substitutes for truth	deceived
Offers crumbs when we can have a banquet	dissatisfied
Keeps us too busy with temporal things	unproductive
Produces double-minded devotion	uncommitted, unfaithful

The cure is to repent (James 4:2-10), say yes to God and no to the devil. Acknowledge sin and be remorseful, humbling oneself; remember that life is short/fragile (vs. 13-15) and do what's right (vs. 17).

It comes down to this: If you live for yourself and your happiness and your pleasures, then you will be a miserable person. It's ironic that the people who live for happiness never find it, while the people who live for God find happiness as a byproduct. The people who chase after pleasure never really experience it—they may find little bits here and there, but nothing to speak of. Yet the people who live for God experience the ultimate pleasure.

"You will show me the way of life, granting me the joy of your presence and pleasures of living with you forever" (Psalm 16:11). True happiness comes from God.[27]

In conclusion, worldliness (loving the world and the things of the world) leads to separation from God (James 4:4), but the reverse is humility, which leads to a restored relationship with God. (James 4:10)

Take a few minutes and quietly examine your heart. Has this lesson convicted you? Is there anyone you need to forgive? Are you living for the pleasures of this world? Does this world have a hold on you? What do you need to forsake? Confess (admit) it to God right now and ask for His help. Jesus

[27] Greg Laurie, *Daily Devotions*, Harvest Ministries, www.harvest.org.

said *"These things I have spoken to you, that in Me you may have peace. In the world you will have tribulation; but be of good cheer, I have overcome the world."* (John 16:33) Jesus can help you be an overcomer!

____

____

____

____

____

Lesson 6
The Armor of God

As we discussed in the previous lesson, the Christian life is a battle. We battle our own fleshly nature, the devil and the world we live in. It is not wise to go into battle unprotected, unprepared or uninformed. We must know who our enemy is and how he operates. We must study his game plan, his tactics and his weaknesses. Much like a ball team studies everything about their opponent; they go into the game "armed" to win.

Who are we at war with according to I Peter 5:8; Ephesians 6:10-20?

____

____

How can we overcome and by whose power? I John 4:4

____

____

What are we instructed to do when attacked? I Peter 5:6-11

____

____

We are at war with the powers of darkness, but God who lives within us is greater. It is vital that we stay plugged into our source of power. The Bible warns us to be on the alert to the devil's tactics, to humble ourselves to

God and to resist the devil in God's power. "Victory is assured to those who know how victory is won and who war accordingly. Satan would love to keep you ignorant, misinformed, or fearful of the subject of spiritual warfare. Jesus said, *"You shall know the truth, and the truth shall set you free"* (John 8:32). Truth is always liberating."[28]

God and His Word is truth. It is vital that we stay in His Word so we are not deceived by the devil. Remember that the devil is the father of lies; he would love to keep us emotionally crippled with lies that we are unworthy, alone, hopeless, unloved, etc. The devil is described as a *"roaring lion"* that roams the earth looking for those he can devour (I Peter 5:8). He is a powerful, sly and deceitful being, but our God is more powerful. We must remember that we cannot stand up to him without God's power. Ephesians 6:11,13 exhorts us to stand firm against his schemes.

Concerning this thing I pleaded with the Lord three times that it might depart from me. And He said to me, "My grace is sufficient for you, for My strength is made perfect in weakness." Therefore most gladly I will rather boast in my infirmities, that the power of Christ may rest upon me. —2 Corinthians 12:8–9

> When you put your faith in Jesus Christ, a sign is effectively hung around your neck that says, "Under new management." You now belong to Jesus Christ, and He does not operate on a timeshare program. Isn't that nice to know? He doesn't say, "Okay, now I have Greg for six months, and the devil can have him for the next six months." That is not what happens. When we put our faith in Christ, He comes in and is the sole resident in our hearts and lives.
>
> Although a Christian cannot be demon-possessed, the devil can affect a Christian outwardly. For instance, demons can tempt and oppress a Christian. The apostle Paul wrote, "And lest I should be exalted above measure by the abundance of the revelations, a thorn in the flesh was given to me, a messenger of Satan to buffet me, lest I be exalted above measure" (2 Corinthians 12:7). The word "buffet" means to hit in the face. So Paul was essentially saying, "Yes, I have come under some demon attack. But here is the good news: God will never give you more than you can handle."

---

[28] Kay Arthur, *LORD is it Warfare?*, p. 13.

> The Bible tells us in James 2:19, "You believe that there is one God. You do well. Even the demons believe—and tremble!" Of course, just because you believe something is true doesn't mean you have committed yourself to it. Obviously, demons are in rebellion against God.
>
> Paul's oppression was allowed by God and orchestrated by Satan. So God may allow the devil to tempt you or harass you in some way. But remember, He won't give you more than you can take. The only thing that will stop the devil is the power of Jesus Christ. He is our only protection. He is the one we need.[29]

The enemy has four primary objectives in interrupting God's work in our lives (Ephesians 6:12). First, Satan wants us to doubt God's Word. The serpent planted a seed of doubt in Eve's mind, and the result was catastrophic for all mankind (Genesis 3:1). Second, Satan tries to distract us from spiritual matters. He wants us focused on earthly, temporary outlets. We get focused on the computer, phone, television or anything with no eternal value. Third, the enemy works to disable us from the Lord's service. Satan will do anything to prevent us from making an impact for Christ. Many popular Christian leaders have fallen into sin and their testimony was completely discredited. Fourth, Satan wants to destroy us physically through illness, stress, obesity, addictions. These things can consume us and cause us to focus on the physical and distract us from the spiritual. Satan uses these tactics to render us useless and ineffective for God. His tactics cause us to be weak in battle. We must be aware of his tactics and armed with the knowledge of God's Word and lean on God's Spirit.[30]

We must also go into battle fully protected and prepared both with offensive as well as defensive weapons. God has prepared a spiritual armor for us and it is our responsibility to put it on daily and use it. Notice that we are told to put on the full armor (not just part of it). Ephesians 6:11

The Equipment - Ephesians 6:13-17

The girdle of ____________________(v. 14a)

The breastplate of ________________(v. 14b)

---

[29] Pastor Greg Laurie, Harvest Daily Devotions, "Within Limits".

[30] Dr. Charles Stanley, *In Touch Daily Devotions*, www.intouch.org.

The shoes of the ________________(v. 15)

The shield of ___________________(v. 16)

The helmet of __________________ (v. 17)

The sword of the ________________(v. 17b)

The armor that protects us in warfare is the girdle of truth, the breastplate of righteousness, the shoes of the Gospel, the shield of faith, the helmet of salvation and the sword of the Spirit. Let's look at each one more closely.

What is the importance of the girdle, breastplate, shield, etc.? Write your thoughts by each piece of equipment.

The girdle of truth ____

Satan is a liar and the father of lies. A Christian must be grounded in the truth so he will not be shaken by falsehood. The girdle holds all the other parts of the armor together. In the same way, the truth is at the core of the believer's life.

The breastplate of righteousness _________________________________

This piece of armor protects all the vital organs. When we accept Christ as savior (He took our sins on Himself at the cross) He clothes us in His righteousness. (2 Corinthians 5:21) It also represents the righteous life of a believer (Ephesians 4:24) that withstands Satan's accusations.

The shoes of the Gospel ______________________________________
The sandals worn by the Roman soldiers had hobnails on the soles. A soldier is only effective if he is steady on his feet. The Gospel shows us how to be at peace with God and we share that with others so they experience the same. A believer has the Gospel to help him stand and be able to withstand the attacks of the enemy.

The shield of faith ______________________________

In our Christian journey we will experience the fiery darts of the enemy (temptation, lies, doubts, fears, discouragements, etc). As we walk by faith (trusting in God's promises and in His power) and use our shield as a defensive weapon, we will be able to extinguish those fiery darts.

The helmet of salvation ______________________________

The battle (and the struggle) is in the mind and that is where Satan attacks. Our minds must be controlled by God. It is harder to be led astray by the enemy when our mind/intellect is established in the scriptures and biblical perspective. As believers we know who we are in Christ (our identity) and our eternal destiny is secure.

The sword of the Spirit ______________________________

The sword is an offensive weapon to use against the enemy. The sword of the Spirit is referring to the Word of God and we can use the Word to defeat the enemy. Jesus quoted scriptures when He was being tempted by Satan in the wilderness. (Luke 4:1-13) He used scriptures as a weapon to silence the devil; James 4:7 tells us to resist the devil and he will flee from us. The Word of God is powerful and will cause the devil to flee. Know it and use it when you are being tempted. Note that the armor protects us from the enemy (the flesh, the devil and the world). Sometimes it is our own fleshly desires that we fight against, sometimes it is the devil, other times it is this world's perspective/mindset.

In what area of your life are you struggling? Where is the enemy warring with you the most? Is it your thought life, your emotions, a sinful habit?

____

____

____

How can you apply the armor of God in that area?

___

___

___

Worry and fear seem to be sins that plague a large number of believers. Let's use worry as an example of how to handle the onslaught of the enemy (same principles apply to fear). In the original Greek, *merimnao*, worry is a combination of two words: *merizo*, which means to divide, and *nous*, which is the mind. Worry means a divided mind. I have to warn you, what you are about to learn is very convicting.

Worry is:[31]
Matthew 6:19-34

Matthew 6:19-25

Matthew 6:25-34

Worry is sin. It is also idolatry. Pride is at the root of worry and anxiety. Worry actually says I'm displeased with God and I need to take over (self-sufficient). The solution is to humbly repent and admit your need.

"Worry is when you're not satisfied in God" – John Piper. It is pushing Him off the throne. "Worry thrives when worship dies". Worry magnifies the problem while worship magnifies God. It also reveals idols of the heart. We don't have idols today, or do we?

Idols are anything or anyone that begins to captive our hearts, minds and affections more than God. It's living on substitutes. The heart is a factory of idols – John Calvin. **The solution is to repent (change of mind that results in a change of behavior) and focus on WORSHIP.**

The third point we see is that worry is unbelief. The solution is faith in God's care, His omniscience (all knowing) and His promises. Read Philippians 4:6-9

[31] Pastor Brad Bigney, *Worry & Fear - The Accepted Sins*, NANC Seminar 2007.

We do this by Right Praying (Phil. 4:6-7) ↦ Right Thinking (Phil. 4:8) ↦ Right Acting (Phil. 4:9). Pour out your heart to God (Psalm 62). Philippians 4:5 is key (worrier needs to know).

Bottom line, worry is a SIN! As a sin, we must STOP excusing it. We MUST confess and repent of it in our lives!

Practically, this is how we can attack the sin of worry (and fear) in our lives.

- Choose 3 verses on God's goodness, care and provision
- Choose 1 song of worship
- Choose 2 people to pray for
- Think of acts of kindness you can do

When thoughts of anxiety or fear come, turn them into worship, prayer and service!

Each time anxious thoughts hit you, **attack them** by doing one of the following:

- reading verses
- minister to someone (do an act of kindness)
- memorize scripture (read and meditate on the verses you chose above)
- sing or hum a song of worship
- intercessory prayer (pray for someone)

Every time you remove a learned behavior, you must replace it with something else. This is the put on/put off principle in Ephesians 4:22-24 where we are exhorted to take off the old man with its sinful behavior and put on Christ by renewing our minds. God's Word is powerful and it renews our minds! Something amazing happens when we redirect our thoughts from worry to thinking about others or when we sing praises or when we remind ourselves of God's goodness and power. You will experience great freedom when you put this into practice. Here are suggested verses to get you started: Joshua 1:9; Psalm 16:8, 11; Psalm 18; Psalm 62.

Apply this to your situation and record your experience below.

____

____

WITNESSING:

HOW DO I SHARE MY FAITH

Lesson 7
Salt & Light

Matthew chapters 5, 6 and 7 are known as the Sermon on the Mount. Jesus is teaching His followers about Kingdom living: what it means to be a child of God and how they are to live. In this Sermon on the Mount, Jesus shares many practical and valuable principles about relationships, priorities, motives, perspectives, etc.

Read Matthew 5:13-16. Jesus tells His followers that they are to be salt and light.

What is significant about salt?

____

____

What is significant about light?

____

____

Salt and light influence everything they come in contact with. Salt changes the flavor of everything it touches. It was used to preserve food and to keep it from spoiling. Salt was a valuable commodity; soldiers in biblical time were sometimes paid in salt. That is where we get the expression "he's not worth his salt".

Light also influences everything around it. Darkness hides, but light exposes and illuminates! Jesus is teaching us that as His follower, we are to influence those around us. We rub shoulders with people every day. Who does your life influence?

What kind of influence are you having on those around you (your family, your co-workers, your neighbors)? Notice that we are to let them see the difference, not for our own praise but for God's. It is easy to complain, be negative or follow the crowd. With God's help, determine in your heart to be a positive and godly influence on others. People are always watching; they will form an impression of you…the question is what type of an impression will it be?

If you are being the kind of Christian that God wants you to be, if you are being a *"salty"* Christian, then your lifestyle will stimulate a thirst for God in others. The greatest compliment is when someone wants to know more, when he or she approaches you and says, "What is it about you?" That is your opportunity to shine the light of the gospel.[32]

Read Colossians 4:6. What does it mean to have our conversation seasoned as with salt? (Hint: the context of this verse is to be gracious in dealing with others)

____

____

____

What are some practical ways that you can influence others for Christ (at home, at school, at work)?

____

____

____

Let each one of you speak truth with his neighbor.

---

[32] Pastor Greg Laurie, Daily Devotions, Harvest Ministries, www.harvest.org.

Ephesians 4:25

Back in 1940, only 20 percent of college students admitted to cheating. Today, that number has increased to 75%-98%. Worse yet, two-thirds of parents think cheating is no big deal and that all students do it, according to statistics from National Public Radio.[1] What has happened to integrity?

In public and private, integrity should guide our lives. There's no better way to silence critics of the Gospel than to live above reproach, according to God's standard of holiness. Nehemiah and the apostle Paul were committed to integrity. As governor of Judah, Nehemiah could have received a food allowance from the Jews. Instead, he fed 150 workers from his own pocket as they rebuilt the Jerusalem wall (Nehemiah 5:14-19). The apostle Paul continued his trade of tent making as he ministered, so that none could misconstrue that he was in ministry for the money (Acts 20:33-35).

If Christians are to influence society toward integrity, we must radiate lives that point people to the Savior through honest living. Perhaps someone is pressuring you to lower your standards - take a stand today and choose a life of integrity.[33]

Truth has no degrees or shades. A half-truth is a whole lie, and a white lie is really black.
John MacArthur

Others can know that when we're around, the environment (around the office, for example) will be positive, helpful, affirming and clean versus negative, complaining, backstabbing and full of sexual innuendos. Sometimes we fail and blow it in our Christian life (i.e. lose our temper, give into temptation, etc). Jesus describes that as being tasteless (ineffective) Matthew 5:13. That is, we lose our ability to influence. God promises to forgive and cleanse us when we come to Him and admit our failures (covered in detail in **Lesson 6** of Christian Journey, Part One: **Staying close to the Vine**).

Read Acts 1:8. What does Jesus say we will be?

____

[33] Dr. David Jeremiah, Turning Point Daily Devotions, Truth-Ful.

What is a witness called to do?

A witness in a court room is asked to tell what he/she saw, heard and experienced. Jesus calls us to be His witnesses. We are to tell others what we know and have experienced in our relationship with God; to share what He has done for us and how He has changed our lives. Look at two passages that illustrate the testimony of a witness.

The woman at the well. John 4: 6-26

What was the response of the woman after she spoke to Jesus? John 4:28-30.

What happened as a result of the woman's witness? John 4:40-42.

In verse 25, we see that she believed in the Messiah and that one day He would come and explain all things (things of God). Jesus talked to her about how to truly worship God (vs. 23). He also revealed personal things to her about her own life (vs.17-18). As a natural response to her encounter with Jesus, she ran and told others to ***"come"*** and ***"see"***.

The blind man. John 9

What was the blind man's simple testimony of what happened to him? John 9:25.

____

The blind man that Jesus healed did not understand everything that happened to him, nor did he understand everything about who Jesus was. He knew one simple thing, he was blind and Jesus gave him sight! **You and I may not understand deep theological things or be an expert in the Bible, but we can tell others what Jesus has done for us and how He has changed our lives.** Notice that in vs. 35-37, when Jesus declared Himself as the Son of Man (referred to as the Christ 9:22, sent from God 9:33), the blind man **believed** and **worshipped**. He showed simple faith.

Jesus made the claim that He is the **"light of the world"** (9:5) right before He restored sight to the blind man. In verse 39 we see a contrast; an amazing statement made by Jesus. He referred to the religious leaders as being spiritually blind (they were to be the experts in the Law but their hearts were far from God). By claiming to be the light of the world, Jesus is teaching that He gives sight to those who are spiritually blind. **Did you know that a person can be religious but not right with God (spiritually blind)?**

When you build relationships, love and serve others, people will be more likely to listen when you talk to them about Christ. (Matthew 5:16) One way to influence others for Christ is to show them how they can have a relationship with Him (this will be covered in detail in the next lesson, Sharing the Gospel). Another way is to share what Christ means to you and what He has done in your life (this is referred to as your personal testimony).

This reminds us that one of the best arguments for the Christian faith is a transformed life. Believers are the best advertising God could have because their lifestyles change, their attitudes change, and even their countenances change. The greatest biography of Jesus is written in the words and actions of His people. Your godly lifestyle is a testimony, just as if you were a walking miracle like the lame man whom Peter and John healed.[34]

Every Christian has a story to tell. What was your life like before you knew Christ, how you came to accept Him as your Savior and then what your life has been like since. This story is called your personal testimony of faith. You will have the opportunity to write your personal testimony in this lesson. As you answer the questions below, keep in mind that this will be something you can share with others in a casual conversation, so try to keep it to about **3-4 minutes**. This is an excellent and effective tool in sharing your faith with others! Stop now and use the blank spaces below to write your testimony, answering the following three questions:

Describe your life before you knew Christ (your lifestyle, relationships, perspective, behavior, etc.)

____

____

____

____

____

____

____

____

____

Describe how you came to faith in Christ (the people, events and scripture God used to draw you to Himself)

[34] Pastor Greg Laurie, *Daily Devotions*, Harvest Ministries, www.harvest.org.

Describe your life after you received Christ (in what ways has your new relationship with Christ changed you; your lifestyle, behavior or attitude?

Choose a verse that God has used in your life and include it in your testimony. (Once you finish your testimony, return to complete this lesson)

I Peter 3:15 exhorts us to be able and ready to share the hope that is in us at any time. I suggest you share your story first with another Christian and as you feel more comfortable and God gives you opportunities, share it with others that do not know Christ. **Share it with kindness and joy. Be careful not to be negative or critical or point out any persons or groups** (your purpose is not to judge or condemn). **Be specific but appropriate** (without giving out intimate personal details). **There is no need to mention specific names, dates or denominations**. Always remember who your audience is; you are talking to unbelievers, so **don't use Christian "lingo"** that they will not understand or that may push them away. Keep it simple and straightforward. **Remember to keep the focus on God and what He has done in your life!**

Jesus told Nicodemus in John 3:3-7 that in order to enter the kingdom of heaven, a man must be born again. We have been born physically (flesh) into this world but we need to be born spiritually in order to enter heaven. This spiritual birth is what happens when we call on God to save us from our sin and accept Christ as our Savior; God cleanses us and transforms our lives through the work of His Holy Spirit that enters and lives within us! How does this happen? How do you then continue living in God's power? Life is hard; how do we access that power for everyday living? Read II Corinthians 2:8-12. How did Paul handle his present difficulties?

____

____

____

John 14:17 says when someone receives Jesus as Savior, His Spirit comes to live inside the new believer. As a result of this "indwelling," the power that Christ demonstrated while on earth prevails in those who now call upon Him for aid. However, for us to access His supernatural strength, we must trust His promise to supply what we need when we need it. As long as we attempt to muddle through using our own abilities, we will prevent

His Spirit from unleashing divine help. Jesus Christ's power is unleashed in our life when we acknowledge our helplessness.[35]

Read Romans 8:11; II Corinthians 6:16; I John 4:13

How are we changed and by whom? Where does He live?

____

____

____

"But when He saw the multitudes, He was moved with compassion for them, because they were weary and scattered, like sheep having no shepherd". (Matthew 9:36) It is not easy to turn a conversation to spiritual things but we are compelled to step out and share our faith with others. Several things compel us: the realization that people are struggling aimlessly through life; they are lost and without hope if they don't have Christ; the reality of a literal place of eternal judgment and torment called hell. Jesus came to earth with the very purpose "to seek and to save that which was lost". (Luke 19:10) Step out by faith and talk to people about their relationship with God.

Religion

Religion does not change a person. Man does not need religion, but a relationship; a relationship with God through Jesus Christ is what transforms a life! You will be surprised to find out that Jesus was not a fan of religion in fact he openly condemned it. He had a lot to say to the religious leaders of His day and in the process offended them to the extent they plotted to destroy Him. (Matthew 15:12; 12:14)

What did Jesus call them in Matthew 3:7; 23:13.

____

____

[35] Dr. Charles Stanley, *In Touch Daily Devotional*, www.intouch.org.

Note some of their characteristics.

Matthew 9:11

____

Matthew 12:2-8

____

Matthew 12:14

____

Matthew 12:24

____

Matthew 12: 38

____

Matthew 15:1-12

____

What did Jesus think of their piety and doctrine?

____

Matthew 23:13-14

Matthew 16:12

Matthew 5:20

Jesus called them brood of vipers and hypocrites. They were arrogant, judgmental, legalistic, and self-righteous. They were also unbelieving demanding a sign, murderers at heart and accusing Jesus of casting out demons by the power of the devil. They ignored God's commands and were teaching the people to follow the traditions of their elders, revealing their wrong doctrine and lost spiritual condition.

Legalism is very sneaky and deceptive; it can creep into our lives very easily. We must be diligent and sober. Search your heart and be very honest with yourself and with God. Are there any such characteristics present in your life today?

Are you willing to name it and to ask God for forgiveness? Are you willing to repent from it (forsake it)?

Jesus calls us to true faith in God; to a transformation of the heart that only comes by knowing Him. He condemns religion that imposes a list of rules but is empty and powerless. It is the grace of God that opens our eyes to this truth and draws us to a relationship with God through Jesus Christ.

Lesson 8
Sharing the Gospel

Sharing our faith in Christ is one of the greatest privileges for a believer, but it can also be a very intimidating experience. Every believer needs to view sharing their faith as a way of life. This lesson will attempt to explain and simplify the process.

Jesus' last words to His disciples in Matthew 28: 18-20 are commonly referred to as the Great Commission. *And Jesus came and spoke to them, saying, "_____ authority has been given to Me in heaven and on earth. ____ therefore and make ________ of all the nations, __________ them in the name of the Father and of the Son and of the Holy Spirit, teaching them to _________ all things that I have ____________ you; and lo, I am with you always, even to the end of the age." Amen*

Every believer is commissioned to **go** and **tell**; it is our spiritual responsibility. Jesus ends with a promise. What is that promise?

____

____

We must view it as simply building relationships and talking to others about their relationship with God. Our goal as a Christian should be to look for ways to share our faith; to turn every day conversations into opportunities to talk about spiritual things with fellow students, co-workers and neighbors. When you get serious about sharing your faith, you will be surprised how God opens doors of opportunities. We don't have to go far before we see a co-worker or a friend experience hardship or pain. Seize the opportunity to reach out to them with assurance of God's love, comfort and of your prayers for them.

In his book Lifestyle Evangelism, Joe Aldrich uses a farming analogy to explain the process of evangelism (sharing our faith) to be three stages:

Cultivation *– an appeal to the heart through the building of relationship*
Sowing *– an appeal to the mind through the communication of revelation*
Reaping *– an appeal to the will in anticipation of a response*

Evangelism is gift-driven. Some are great cultivators, some are gifted sowers, while others are gifted reapers. Furthermore, our Lord made it clear that evangelism is a process. He told His disciples, *"I'm sending you out to reap (stage 3) what you haven't sown."* Others had done the hard labor (John 4:37-38). Cultivators should not feel like they failed if they do not reap. *"I have planted, Apollos watered but God gave the increase"*. God is our joint-venture partner in this process of cultivating, sowing and reaping (I Corinthians 3:6).[36]

Effective evangelism begins where people are and not where we would like them to be. As the king's messengers, our challenge is to help others discover how their needs can be satisfied through a relationship with Jesus Christ.[37] Look for the pressing needs in their life: is it a troubled marriage, coping with illness, struggling with finances, experiencing guilt or a terrible addiction; whatever their need, direct them to the One who can help them and can give them peace. **Show them how a relationship with Christ is relevant to their lives!**

Dennis and Barbara Rainey sum it up well in their devotional book, Moments for Couples. (Though this is directed towards children, it is basic truth which applies to all)

> *But what does a child, or any person, need to know to become a Christian? The following are the basics: First, children need to be taught who God is and how He loves them. They need to know what sets Him apart from humans. God is holy; He is perfect. People, however, are not perfect. God is just; He is always fair. We are not just in all our decisions. God is love; He desires a relationship with us. That's why He sent His Son. We are not always motivated out of our love for another.*
>
> *Second, children need to be taught that their sins must be forgiven (see Rom. 6:23). Many parents in this culture of tolerance feel*

---

[36] Joe Aldrich, *Lifestyle Evangelism*, 1993, p. 77.

[37] Ibid, p. 85.

uncomfortable talking about hell. God is patient, but He is not tolerant. His justice calls for an atonement (a payment, a penalty) for people's sins. Our children must have some understanding that their sins can keep them out of heaven. Their sins must be paid for. And that is what Jesus Christ did for us on the cross.

Finally, children need to know that they receive God's forgiveness through faith in Jesus Christ (see Eph. 2:8,9).

Faith involves repenting of our sins, turning to God in faith and trusting Jesus Christ to be our Savior and Lord. When we repent, we acknowledge our sins before God and express our sorrow about our sins to Him.

The following scripture verses takes a person through a progressive understanding of **God's love, man's sinful state and God's provision of forgiveness (through the blood of Christ on the cross)**. These are the basic truths that need to be communicated. I challenge you to commit these verses to memory. Read each passage and summarize.

John 3:16

____

____

Romans 3:23

____

____

Romans 6:23

____

____

Romans 5:8

____

____

Ephesians 2:8-9

____

____

Romans 10:9

____

____

II Corinthians 5:17

____

____

There are no magic words to pray when we accept Christ, but it is important that the individual understands his sinfulness, his need for salvation and acknowledge Jesus as Savior. It is also important that people understand that it is their faith in what Christ has done for them on the cross that saves them and not any religious or external work they have done. The gift of salvation and eternal life is given freely to all who come to God by faith in Christ. Once a person comes to understand the basic truths of his need for God's salvation, you can walk him through a simple prayer such as this.

Dear God, I have sinned and broken your laws. I ask for your forgiveness. I believe Jesus died on the cross for my sins. I receive Him as my Lord and Savior.

It is good for us to remember that it is God's responsibility to save and not our own. Our responsibility is to share the Gospel, the good news. God works in a person's heart to convict them of their sin, to show them their need for Christ and to draw them to Himself. God calls us to be His witnesses; He expects us to share with people what He has done in our own lives and how He can do the same for them.

One of the most powerful ways to share Christ is to simply talk about what He means to you and what He has done in your life. Sharing your personal testimony is closely related to this (your personal story of how you came to faith in Jesus Christ). Sharing what He means to you or your personal testimony should flow naturally in conversation. Practice it so that it becomes natural.

You can also share verses out of the Bible, or you can use a Bible tract like **Do you want to know God personally?** (formerly The Four Spiritual Laws by Dr. Bill Bright, Founder and President of Campus Crusade for Christ). This tract is a simple and effective way of going through the Gospel. You simply read through it with them (eliminates the uncertainty of what to say). It also presents the individual with the opportunity to pray and invite Christ into their life.

Other ways to use tracts can be to leave them with a tip at a restaurant, in a break room or send in a card; pray about creative ways and places. Also, don't forget to pray for those that will be finding and reading those tracts.

As stated before, sharing the Gospel and winning people to Christ is a process called evangelism. Joe Alrich in his book Lifestyle Evangelism talks about four enemies of effective evangelism. Look at the following chapters and see if you can spot them and write a summary of each.

Matthew 16 (two elements found here)

I Corinthians 5

___

Galatians 5

___

These elements can be in a church or an individual's life. They are: hypocrisy, rationalism, impurity and legalism.[38] Use the space below to write out a definition of each.

___

___

___

___

___

___

We can see that having any of these present in our lives (or church) can quench the power of God and as a result hinder our effectiveness to reach others for Christ.

Let your behavior back up what you say. Let your walk match your talk! No one likes a hypocrite. Has your life changed since you have come to know Christ? Do people see Jesus in you? The apostle Paul persecuted Christians, but this is what was said about him after his conversion, *But they were hearing only, "He who formerly persecuted us now preaches the faith which he once tried to destroy." And they glorified God in me.* (Galatians 1:23-24)

[38] Joe Aldrich, *Lifestyle Evangelism*, pp. 116-129.

Instead, develop these divine signposts: love, unity, good works and hope; these will lead a nonbeliever toward the foot of the cross.[39] In the lives of Christians, these qualities can be very attractive to those who are without Christ.

Are you making a difference in anyone's life? Are you making a difference in your home, office, school or neighborhood? Don't make winning them to Christ the only goal. They can sense if you don't truly care about them (it's about building a relationship, loving and serving people).

Write down three names of people you would like to share Christ with. Begin praying for opportunities to talk with them. In the meantime, look for ways to build a relationship with them (initiate conversations, invite them out for lunch or golfing, have them over for a cookout or a fun activity, etc.). Write down some ideas below.

____

____

____

____

____

____

How about you? Do people praise God because of you? Are you making a difference in your part of the world? God has called you and placed you where you are for a reason. Are you glorifying him and pleasing him in your Christian walk? Are you a doer of the word? (James 1:22) Write down your thoughts and any changes you need to make in your life.

____

____

---

[39] Ibid, p. 123.

Before wrapping up this lesson, I want to emphasize one more point. It is often the case that we lead people to faith in Christ and leave them in that infant stage. They are left to flounder and figure out the rest for themselves (or fall away).

Before returning to heaven, Jesus commissioned His disciples with these words, *"All authority has been given to Me in heaven and on earth, Go therefore and make disciples of all the nations, baptizing them in the name of the Father and of the Son and of the Holy Spirit, teaching them to observe all things that I have commanded you; and lo, I am with you always, even to the end of the age."* (Matthew 28:18-20) Once a person comes to faith in Christ, it is vital they get plugged into a local church and become discipled by a mature believer.

It is a sad thing to come to Christ and remain a babe in the faith; just like physical and emotional growth is important, so is spiritual growth. A study such as this one can provide the spiritual knowledge (foundation) needed to grow up in Christ. Growth comes through studying the Word of God, the Bible and learning other disciplines such as prayer and service. "... as **newborn** babes, desire the pure milk of the word, that you may grow thereby". (1 Peter 2:2)

I Peter 2:4-6 and Ephesians 2:19-22 speak of the importance of this growth process. Look up these passages and write what you learn. Who is our foundation and how are we being built up?

____

...having been built on the foundation of the apostles and prophets, Jesus Christ Himself being the chief cornerstone, (Ephesians 2:20)

But you are a ________ generation, a ________ priesthood, a ______ nation, His own ________ people, that you may proclaim the praises of Him who called you out of darkness into His marvelous light; who once were not a people but are now the people of God, who had not obtained mercy but now have obtained mercy. (I Peter 2:9-10)

This is your identity in Christ. What does this mean to you? How does it change your thinking or behavior?

____

____

____

____

____

We are being built up to be a spiritual house and a holy people; we are the people of God, representing Him here on earth.

Suggested Reading
Witnessing without Fear by Dr. Bill Bright
Life Style Evangelism by Joe Alrich
Becoming A Contagious Christian by Mark Mittelberg, Lee Strobel, Bill Hybels

SECOND COMING:

HOW CAN I BE PREPARED

Lesson 9
The Bride of Christ

The Bible refers to the church as the Body of Christ; many members but one body. The church is also called the Bride of Christ. Jesus called Himself the bridegroom and the church His bride (Revelation 18:23; 21:9; Matthew 9:15). This takes on a whole new meaning and depth when we consider the ancient Jewish wedding traditions. In this lesson we will look at the beauty of the parallel between the ancient Jewish wedding traditions and the spiritual aspect of Christ the bridegroom and His bride the church.

There are three phases in the ancient Jewish marriage experience. The arrangement, the betrothal and the celebration phase. Notice they begin with ABC, which will help us to remember them.[40]

The first phase is the arrangement or the *shiddukhin*. During this phase the potential bride was identified, the details of the arrangements were negotiated and the betrothal covenant was ratified.[41] Part of the arrangements is the price to be paid, a dowry, for the bride.

The second phase is the betrothal, or the *kiddushin*, which is from a Hebrew root word meaning *"sanctified"* or *"set apart."*[42] This phase was an important time of preparation for the marriage relationship as well as the upcoming wedding celebration. This period is marked by physical and spiritual preparation as the bride and the bridegroom set themselves apart exclusively for each other. Although similar to a modern day engagement, the ancient Jewish betrothal was a more permanent arrangement that could be terminated only by death or divorce.[43]

The third phase is the celebration, or the *nissuin*, usually occurring about one year after the betrothal. This final phase is marked with the bridegroom's return for his bride and a great wedding celebration.[44]

We will take each phase and see the parallel to Christ and His bride, the church.

---

[40] Martha Lawley, Attending the Bride - Preparing for His Return, 2005, p. 13.

[41] Barney Kasdan, God's appointed Customs (Baltimore: Lederer Books, 1996), p. 48.

[42] Ibid, p. 12

[43] Ibid, p. 6

[44] Lawley, p. 13; Kasdan, p. 13.

Read each reference below and identify the characters.

Matthew 22:1-2

____

John 3:22-30; Mark 2:18-20

____

II Corinthians 11:2; Ephesians 5:22-32

____

Matthew 25:1-13; Matthew 22:13

____

The characters are: the father, the bridegroom, the bride and the attendants.

It's important for us to understand that the 10 virgins in this parable are bridal attendants that are waiting for the bridegroom to return from his father's house to claim his bride. The parable refers to believers as attendants to the bride of Christ, emphasizing the importance of individual responsibility in preparing for the bridegroom's return. Christ assigns to every Christian personal responsibility in helping to prepare the bride for His coming. (ABC) We play dual roles; we are part of the bride (the church) as well as attendants to the bride.

The Arrangement phase[45]

- The father of the bridegroom identifies the bride, extends the offer of relationship, negotiates the terms and makes the arrangements. How does this relate to our relationship with God? (John 3:16-18; 14:6)

[45] Lawley, p. 19

- There was a price paid for the bride. (1 Peter 1:18-19) What did Christ pay for His bride?

- The covenant is made between the bridegroom and the bride. What covenant is made between Christ and the church? (John 10: 28; 14:2-3)

- God gave us a man that identifies us as His. What identifies us as belonging to God? (II Corinthians 1:21-22)

The Father draws us to a relationship with Himself through His Son Jesus Christ. In order to reconcile us to Himself, our debt of sin had to be paid. He paid it by the blood of His Son on the cross at Calvary. When we believe in Him and accept God's gift of forgiveness, we come into a relationship with Him. This relationship is a covenant or a promise of eternal life, and one day He will return to take us home to live with Him forever. In the meantime, God gave us the Holy Spirit as a mark that we belong to Him. The Bible says that we have been sealed by the Holy Spirit. (Ephesians 1:13-14)

The Betrothal phase[46]

- The bridegroom returns to his father's house to prepare a place for his bride. What did Jesus go to do? (John 14:6)

  ____

  ____

- The bride prepares for her groom's return. Who is described as the radiant bride? (Ephesians 5:25-27)

  ____

  ____

- How is the bride dressed and what does it represent? (Isaiah 61:10; Revelation 19:8)

  ____

  ____

- How is the church to prepare for her bridegroom's return? (II Corinthians 3:18; 11:2, Hebrews 1:3)

  ____

  ____

- The bride and her groom are to remain faithful to one another; they are considered officially married at this stage. How does the church remain holy and faithful to her bridegroom/Savior? (I Thessalonians 5:23-24)

---

[46] Ibid, p. 54

- Individuals attend to the bride as she prepares herself. Likewise, individual believers attend to the church through the help of the Holy Spirit. As the Holy Spirit leads and gives strength, believers serve Christ in the local church. This service builds up the church by building up its people. Note how this takes place. (Ephesians 2:21; Jude 1:20; I Corinthians 3:9)

Just as the bridegroom works with his father to prepare, Jesus works with His Father to prepare a place in His house for us. (John 14:1-3) While the bridegroom is away, the bride prepares herself. Believers are called to live pure lives and allow God's Spirit to transform them in the image of Christ. Our time on earth is a preparation for eternity; for the time when we join our bridegroom in our heavenly home that He is preparing for us. This time of spiritual preparation is parallel to the bride preparing her wedding garments and awaiting her bridegroom's return for her.

The Celebration phase[47]

- The father of the bridegroom determines when it's time to send his son to claim his bride and to begin the celebration. Read the wedding parable in Matthew 22:1-10. Notice, it is the father that summons the guests to the wedding celebration. (Matt 22:2-3) Our heavenly Father calls to all who will come; sadly, not all will accept His invitation. To all who accept, He gives eternal life.

- The trumpet will sound. In the Old Testament, a shofar or trumpet was used to summon the people to worship, to a celebration, or to a call to war. What will happen when the final trumpet sounds? (I Thessalonians 4:16-17)

[47] Lawley, p. 130

____

____

- The wedding celebration

We will meet Jesus in the air and He will gather His church to live with Him forever.

Read Revelation 19:6-9 and see the spiritual parallel. There will be unspeakable joy when Jesus comes back for the church; the celebration event is known as the marriage supper of the Lamb. The Lamb is the Son of God, Jesus Christ, being united with His bride, the church. He loved her and gave His life for her, and now she will live with Him for eternity.

Are you preparing yourself for your bridegroom? Our time on earth is preparation for heaven and eternity. The Bible likens the Christian life to a race. God desires that we run well, getting rid of anything that weighs us down (sin, distractions), and remain focused on the prize that is waiting for us. That prize represents living and serving in a way that pleases God.

Read I Corinthians 9:24-27. Life is a race you and I must finish … and win. Dennis Rainey shares five different kinds of runners and the great analogy to the Christian life.

The Casual Runner. He runs when he feels like it. For this Christian, the sacrifice demanded by the race is just too high.

The Cautious Runner. He thinks a lot about the race, but he plays it safe and seldom leaves the starting blocks.

The Compromised Runner. Unwilling to lay aside present pleasures, he has given into temptations to run outside his prescribed lane. He has few convictions and takes no costly stands in life.

The Callous Runner. This veteran runner is a cynic and is critical of people. Preoccupied with his injuries, his heart contains layers of thick, tough tissue made of bitterness, envy or apathy.

The Committed Runner. This person is determined to win and knows where the finish line is. "In training" at all times, he knows victory is never achieved by the fainthearted.

What kind of runner are you? How do you run to win? According to the Apostle Paul: you must exercise self-control in all things. The discipline of our desires is the backbone of character. Know what tempts you and avoid it.

Know where you are going. Keep your eyes on Jesus. Grow in Him and live to please Him.

Be willing to sacrifice your own rights, plans and agenda. We are called to die to ourselves; those who lose their life for His sake will find it (Matthew 16:25).[48]

Take a few minutes and examine your heart. Are there any changes you need to make?

____

____

____

____

What does it mean to be disqualified from the race according to I Corinthians 9:27? How can one be disqualified?

____

____

____

[48] Dennis and Barbara Rainey, *Moments Together for Couples*, Running to Win (Part One & Two).

We can live in sin and willful disobedience to God and His Word (it's dangerous to reject God's leading). We can live as rebellious children full of pride and refusing to repent; this dishonors God and ruins our Christian testimony before others.

Living in sin, also affects the whole Body of Christ; our sin does not only affect us but it has a ripple effect. A little leaven leavens the whole lump. (Galatians 5:19) Leaven in the Bible is a symbol of sin. In other words, a little sin in our life will affect our whole life and the lives of others. It's "the little foxes that spoil the vines". (Song of Solomon 2:15) Don't miss the small things; in other words, it's the little things that spoil a person's character. It starts with one drink, one magazine, one internet site, one night; then it becomes a habit and then a stronghold. We must live blameless lives even in the little things; otherwise we will no longer be useful or useable by God.

Lesson 10
God's Plan for the Ages

The most important question about Heaven is, *How do I get there?* Contrary to popular opinion, entrance isn't based on good works, high morals, church attendance, baptism, or membership in the "right" denomination. It centers on the person of Jesus Christ. If we acknowledge we're sinners separated from God, receive Jesus' sacrificial death as payment for our rebellion, and trust Him as Savior and Lord, we instantly become a child of God. Then, a place in Heaven is reserved for us. Are you sure you're Heaven-bound?[49]

This topic of God's plan and order of events is extremely complicated and controversial. Among Christians and scholars alike, there are differing views as to what will happen, how it will happen and when it will happen. This lesson is meant to only be a survey of God's plan for the ages; the purpose for this lesson is to give you a **very brief overview** and to **highlight** the major points/events. As you go through this lesson, place each event in history on the time line provided in the back of the lesson. When you have finished, refer to the completed timeline provided for you (but don't look ahead).

The Rapture of the Church

The term rapture is not found in the Bible but the idea is; rapture means to catch or snatch away. After His resurrection, Jesus made promises to His followers that He will return one day and take them to be with Him forever. (John 14:1-3)

Read the following passages and record the details.

John 13:1-3

---

[49] Charles Stanley, *In Touch Daily Devotional*, www.intouch.org.

Philippians 3:20

____

I Thessalonians 4:13

____

The trumpet will sound and the Lord Jesus will descend. Those who died in Christ will rise first and then those living believers will meet the **Lord in the air**. Note that the Lord will not come on the earth at this time (His second coming is at a later date).

The Judgment Seat of Christ

It is important for us to understand that this judgment is for the believers and it is not a judgment for sins (that was paid for on the cross) but for rewards. Look up the following and record what you learn.

Romans 14:10

____

I Corinthians 3:9-15

____

II Corinthians 5:10

____

Believers in Christ will be judged according to what they did with the time, talents and resources God had given them on earth. What we have belongs to God; the Bible calls us stewards of those things. Those who have trusted Christ as their Savior but did nothing more for Him, will stand ashamed on that day; they will receive no rewards.

The Marriage of the Lamb

In our previous lesson on the Bride of Christ, we learned that one day the Lord Jesus Christ (our bridegroom) will return for the church (His bride). There will be a great celebration at that time!

Read and note details about the celebration in Revelation 19:7-9.

____

____

The Tribulation

The tribulation period is prophesied in the book of Daniel and is also talked about in the book of The Revelation. This is a period of seven years here on the earth. The first three and one half years is a time of political and world peace but the second half (the Great Tribulation) is described as a terrible time of war and the judgment of God upon the earth.

The first half of the tribulation period is characterized by a political world leader coming to power, known as the Anti-Christ, also referred to as the _______ (Revelation 13:1-2), *the man of*_________, *the*__________ *one* (II Thessalonians 2:3, 8). At first he will appear as a great leader that brings peace and unity to all the nations of the world. He will set up a one world government as well as a one world church. He will win the hearts of all the people and will be viewed as a god with supernatural abilities, but he will be the embodiment of Satan!

The second half, the Great Tribulation is marked by <u>seven</u> seals, trumpets and vials (bowls).

<u>Seals</u> <u>(Revelation 6)</u> world's greatest dictator (1-2), war (3-4), famine, death blow (7-8), persecution (9-11), ecological disaster (12-17), hour of fear (8:1).

Trumpets (Revelation 8, 9) world's greatest fire (7), oceanic disturbance (10-11), pollution of water (12-17), darkness (12-13), pestilence (9:1-12), army (9:13-21), storm (11:15-19).

Bowls (Revelation 16) world's greatest epidemic ((2), contamination by blood (3-7), contamination by blood (cont.), scorching by heat (8-9), plague (10-11), invasion (12-16), destruction (17-21). This terrible period on earth will end with the Battle of Armageddon (Rev 16:16).

The Second Coming of Jesus Christ

The Lord Jesus Christ will descend to earth on the Mount of Olives. (Zechariah 14) Read the passages below and note the details of His coming.

Zechariah 14:3-4

____

Matthew 24:27-31

____

Revelation 19:11-21

____

Note the purpose for Jesus' coming, who His army consists of and what He came to do.

Revelation 19: 7, 8, 14

____

Revelation 19:19-21

____

Matthew 24: 31

____

Matthew 25:31-34

____

Joel 2:1-11 (The Day of the Lord)

____

This time, the Lord Jesus Christ comes to earth to defeat the Antichrist and his armies assembled at Armageddon; He defeats them by the sword (the Word of God). He brings with Him an army of angels and of the saints of God (Christ followers). Jesus comes to restore faithful Israel as well as judge and punish faithless Israel. He also comes to separate the sheep from the goats (this judgment is of those that are alive on the earth at the time, not to be mistaken by the Great White Throne Judgment of those who have died).

The Final Revolt of Satan

Read Revelation 20:2-3.

What are some names for Satan?

____

____

What significant event occurs at this time and for how long?

____

Satan, also known as the devil, the dragon, serpent of old, was bound and thrown in the abyss for a thousand years. This thousand year period is referred to as the Millennium.

Imagine this world without the influence and work of the devil. As hard as it is to imagine, there will be those who live during the Millennium who will reject Christ as their leader and king. This shows that even in a perfect environment, man's heart will not always choose God.

What happens after the thousand years according to Revelation 20:7-10?

____

____

Satan never gives up. Once released, he regains his forces against God and His followers in a final revolt. Notice the word *"deceived"*. Jesus called the devil a liar and the father of lies; his work has always been to deceive and lead people to their destruction.

Praise God that the devil will only be released *"for a little time"* and then he will be thrown into the lake of fire **forever**.

The Great White Throne Judgment

"And as it is appointed for men to die once, but after this the judgment," (Hebrews 9:27)

So far we have seen that the Bible talks of several judgments. When people think of "judgment day", they are referring to this event in history.

Revelation 20:11-15; Daniel 7:9-10; Romans 2:15-16 gives us details concerning this judgment. Record your findings.

Who is the Judge? (John 5:22, 27; II Timothy 4:1)

What will be judged?

Romans 2:15
Matthew 12:36-37
Romans 2:16; Ecclesiastes 12:14
II Corinthians 11:15; Matthew 16:27
Exodus 32:32-33; Philippians 4:3; Revelation 13:8

This is the judgment of all those who have **rejected** Jesus Christ; those whose names were not written in the Book of Life. (Revelation 13:8) These are *"those who sleep"* (the dead) raised up for their final judgment. (John

5:29; Daniel 12:2) This takes place after Satan has been cast into the lake of fire. (Revelation 20:9) The Lord Jesus Christ sits on the throne and judges according to conscience, words, secrets, public works and the Book of Life. (Revelation 22:12, 16)

The Eternal State

One pastor titled his message on this topic *"Home At Last!"*

The last two chapters of Revelation reveal details on the new heaven and new earth.

Read Revelation 21:1-5 and note what will be present and what will be absent.

____

____

Write a description of this place according to Revelation 21:10-27.

____

____

____

____

All the first things will pass away; the first earth and first heaven, the sea, death, mourning, tears and pain. Notice the absence of sin and the presence of only those whose names are written in the Lamb's Book of Life (21:27). A beautiful new and holy city of God referred to as the New Jerusalem will come down from heaven, adorned as a bride. God Himself will dwell among His people and He will be the only light necessary to illuminate the city (22:5). The New Jerusalem is described as having 12 gates (one for each of the tribes of Israel), streets of gold, a wall of jasper and precious stones.

Read Revelation 21:5-7; 12-17; 22:6-7.

How does Jesus describe Himself?

____

____

How does He describe the believers and what does He promise them?

____

____

How does He describe the unbelievers and what does He promise will happen to them?

____

____

What is Jesus' final message?

____

____

Jesus is seated on the throne in heaven (a mark of His kingship and authority) and He describes Himself as the Alpha and the Omega, the beginning and the end, the root of David (Messianic line). He gives life freely to all who will come to Him. He describes believers as those who washed their robes

(sins have been forgiven), have the right to the tree of life and will enter by the gates into the New Jerusalem. The unbelievers are described as dogs (without character), sorcerers, the immoral, murders, idolaters (worship other gods) and those who love and practice lying (habitual sins and refuse Christ's invitation to salvation).
He is the bright and morning star (exalted). Are you looking forward to His return? Are you ready? Live your life in a way that honors Him so you will not be ashamed when you meet Him face to face. He is coming quickly and is bringing His reward *"to give to every one according to his work"*. (Revelation 22:12)

However we speak wisdom among those who are mature, yet not the wisdom of this age, nor of the rulers of this age, who are coming to nothing. But we speak the wisdom of God in a mystery, the hidden wisdom which God ordained before the ages for our glory, which none of the rulers of this age knew; for had they known, they would not have crucified the Lord of glory. But as it is written: *"Eye has not seen, Nor ear heard, Nor have entered into the heart of man The things which God has prepared for those who love Him."* (I Corinthians 2:6-9)

Reflect on what you learned in this lesson and write down your thoughts below. How does knowing these truths effect how you live today?

____

____

____

____

God's Plan for the Ages

∞

∞

God's Plan for the Ages

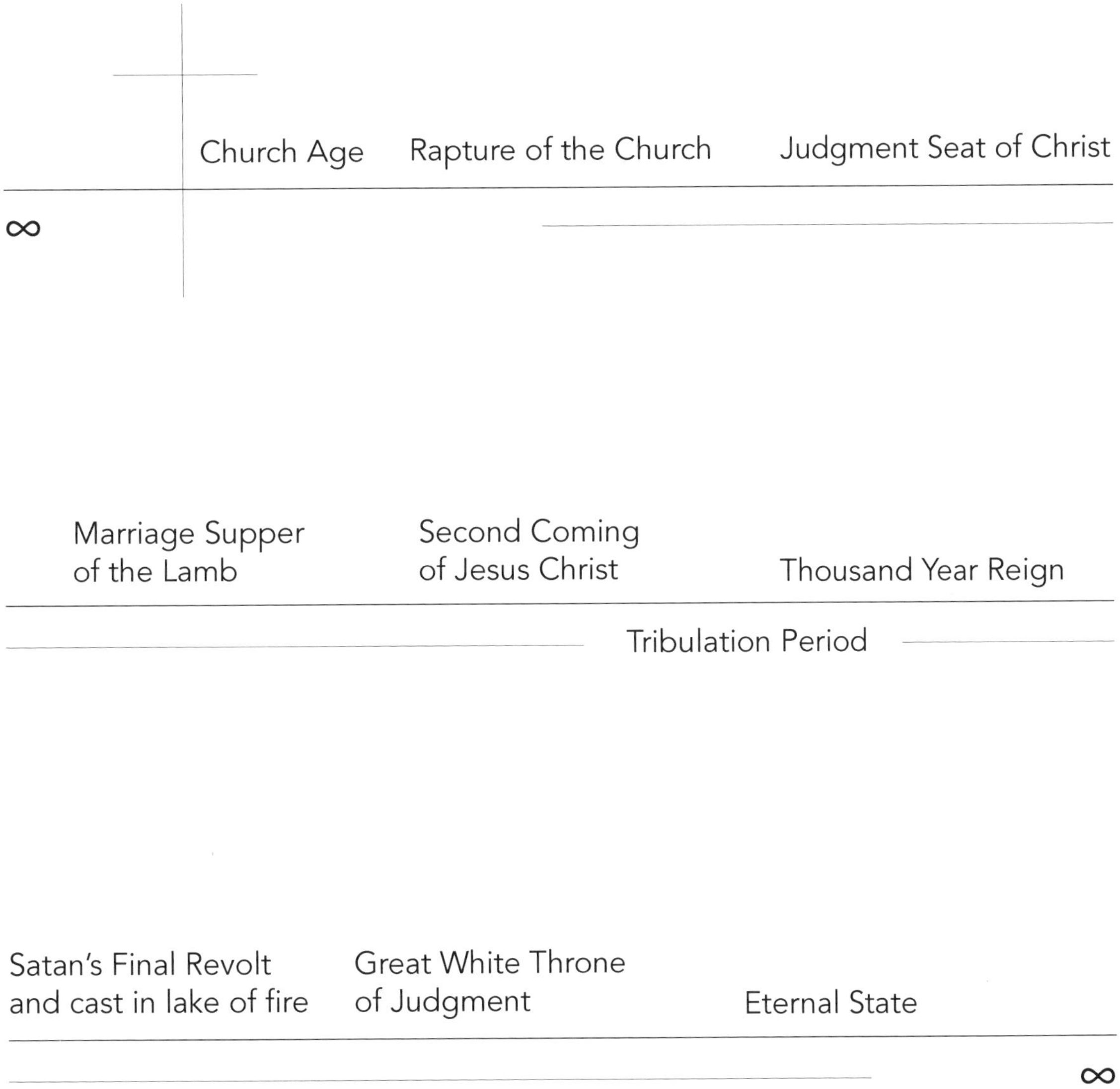

∞

Church Age

Rapture of the Church

Judgment Seat of Christ

Marriage Supper of the Lamb

Second Coming of Jesus Christ

Thousand Year Reign

Tribulation Period

Satan's Final Revolt and cast in lake of fire

Great White Throne of Judgment

Eternal State

∞

Spiritual Gifts Survey

Read the statements one at a time and DO NOT READ AHEAD. Determine your answer based on the 0-3 scoring criteria below and enter it in the numbered box that corresponds with the numbered statement. It is important to respond to the statements based on who you are now and not who you would like to be or think you should be. After you have answered all the questions, total each column with your score.

0 = I am seldom or never this way
1 = I am usually NOT this way
2 = I am this way some of the time
3 = I am this way most or all of the time

1	2	3	4	5	6	7	8	9	10	11	12	13	14
15	16	17	18	19	20	21	22	23	24	25	26	27	28
29	30	31	32	33	34	35	36	37	38	39	40	41	42
43	44	45	46	47	48	49	50	51	52	53	54	55	56
57	58	59	60	61	62	63	64	65	66	67	68	69	70
71	72	73	74	75	76	77	78	79	80	81	82	83	84
Total													
A	**B**	**C**	**D**	**E**	**F**	**G**	**H**	**I**	**J**	**K**	**L**	**M**	**N**

Total your scores for each column and list your highest and lowest three gifts.

Highest gifts

1. ______________________

2. ______________________

3. ______________________

Lowest gifts

1. ______________________

2. ______________________

3. ______________________

1. I like to organize & plan
2. I want to spend time with unbelievers so I can share my faith
3. I enjoy sharing my counsel or being an encourager to others
4. It is important to me that money I give to the church be used as effectively as possible
5. I am motivated more by meeting a need than by doing a task
6. I enjoy using my home to minister to others
7. I can easily get others to complete a ministry project
8. Those who are distressed or elated seem drawn to me
9. I seem to be able to notice sin before others are aware of it
10. I enjoy routine work for church that others find tedious
11. I have a burden to disciple others so they can help others
12. I am able to instruct others in the exact meaning of words & passages in Scripture
13. I like to challenge people's perspective of God through various forms of art
14. I am often sought out for advice on spiritual or personal matters
15. I finish projects & make decisions with great speed
16. Witnessing is the most important task given to Christians
17. I give practical, step-by-step advice to those in need
18. I watch my finances closely so that I can give freely to God's work
19. I prefer to be led by others
20. Guests say they feel comfortable in my home
21. Often groups I'm involved with look to me for leadership
22. I enjoy doing kind deeds for people who cannot or will not return them
23. I am compelled to unmask other people's sins
24. I enjoy doing repetitive tasks for the glory of God
25. I feel the need to protect those whom I disciple
26. I am able to make difficult Bible verses understandable

27. I like to develop & use my artistic skills (art, drama, music, photography, etc.)
28. I can often find simple, practical solutions in the midst of conflict or confusion
29. I enjoy setting goals & then making plans to meet them
30. I urgently feel that a decision for Christ be made when I witness to someone
31. I am more interested in studying Bible passages for practical applications than for deep theological truth
32. It is fun for me to give freely because I love God
33. I rapidly meet other people's need for help
34. I have the ability to make strangers feel at ease
35. I have the ability to make decisions rapidly & stand by them
36. I like visiting those in hospitals & nursing homes
37. I boldly tell others about evils in our government & other worldly systems
38. I like being asked to do jobs at church
39. I deny myself in order to help weak or new Christians
40. Others have told me that I have assisted them in learning biblical truth in a meaningful way
41. I enjoy helping people understand God & their relationship with Him through artistic expression
42. I can easily select the most effective course of action from among several alternatives
43. I volunteer to organize others when I sense a lack of organization
44. I am drawn to unbelievers because I want to win them to Christ
45. Teaching that can't be applied bothers me
46. I am willing to do without in order to give money for God's kingdom
47. I enjoy helping those in leadership by completing some of their smaller tasks so they can minister
48. I enjoy giving food & lodging to those in need
49. I easily adapt my guidance to fit the maturity level of those working with me
50. I want to comfort Christians who are sick or in distress

51. I enjoy being used by God to teach & caution large groups of believers
52. I like projects that require a hands-on approach
53. I care more about relationships than tasks
54. I enjoy spending a lot of time studying the Bible so I can share its truths with others
55. I enjoy looking for new & fresh ways of communicating spiritual truths
56. I can anticipate the likely consequences of an individual's or group's action
57. I thrive on organizing people, ideas, and resources to improve the efficiency of a ministry
58. I have an overwhelming desire to share with unbelievers
59. I like assisting others in resolving difficult problems in their lives
60. I notice when others have a material or financial need
61. I find contentment in helping someone who can use my abilities
62. I like having people visit my home
63. If a group doesn't have a leader, I will lead it
64. I like doing special things for people who are sick or having difficulties
65. I yearn for hearers to be convicted after I have proclaimed God's Word
66. I consider myself a task-oriented person
67. I like being given the job of discipling a group of believers
68. I find contentment studying God's Word & communicating my understanding with others
69. I like to apply different artistic expressions to communicate spiritual truth to others
70. I have insights into how to solve problems that others do not see; I give practical advice to help others thru complicated situations
71. I have put effective plans into place to meet group goals
72. I enjoy meeting non-Christians, even total strangers

73. I enjoy assisting others who are experiencing problems by giving them practical advice
74. I trust God to meet all my needs so that I can give sacrificially of my income
75. I like helping others just because they need me, not because I expect something in return
76. I enjoy welcoming guests & making them feel comfortable
77. I have the ability to help groups of all sizes make decisions
78. I am greatly concerned about comforting others
79. I want my instructions to cause others to see what God says & to respond to His guidance
80. I prefer to follow rather than to lead
81. I desire to care for the spiritual well-being of a group of Christians over an extended time
82. I prefer to compile my own teaching material rather than to present another teacher's material
83. I am creative & imaginative; I regularly need to get alone to reflect & develop my imagination
84. I can supply scriptural truth that others regard as practical & helpful

Spiritual Gifts Key & Analysis

A - Administration
B - Evangelism
C - Exhortation
D - Giving
E - Helps
F - Hospitality
G - Leadership
H - Mercy
I - Prophecy
J - Service
K - Shepherding
L - Teaching
M - Creative Communication
N - Wisdom

Administration – Persons gifted in the area of administration are goal-and objective-oriented. They often have strong organizational skills and are able to coordinate resources to accomplish tasks quickly. They are motivated by accomplishing desired tasks and often derive great satisfaction from viewing the results of what they have accomplished. If you scored high in this area, you should consider being involved in an area of ministry in which you can utilize your organizational strengths to carry out the church's measurable goals. (Measurable goals are objectives such as numerical growth ministries advance, missions expansion). Cautions: be flexible to adjusting your plans; be concerned about people & not only use them to accomplish goals; don't fail to see God's purposes in the process of meeting a goal. I Corinthians 12:28

Evangelism – Persons gifted in the area of evangelism have a strong desire to share the gospel with non-believers in every situation and by all possible means. Their greatest joy in ministry is seeing the unsaved won to Christ. They have a deep desire to fulfill the Great Commission's evangelistic emphasis and prefer to devote more time and effort to the ministry of evangelism than to other church ministries that are for the edification of believers. These persons look for areas where the need for the gospel is greatest and are willing to make personal sacrifices to share the gospel. If you scored high in this area, you should consider being involved in a ministry that places great emphasis on sharing the gospel with the unsaved and reaching out to the un-churched. Cautions: of quenching the Spirit in others, being demanding or pessimistic, moving forward without affirmation or being sent by the church. Acts 8:35

Exhortation – Persons gifted in the area of exhortation have a special ability to encourage others in the body of Christ by giving them words of comfort, encouragement, and counsel in times of need. They are attracted to individuals seeking spiritual growth and often are willing to share their past personal failures to help motivate others toward greater spiritual maturity. Persons gifted in exhortation can make accurate assessments of people's spiritual needs and have the ability to explain truth logically, giving step-by-step instructions that are easy to follow. If you scored high in this area, you should consider being involved in an area where you can use your strengths to minister one-on-one to people in need. Cautions: in being overly optimistic, flattering or simplistic; not taking time to understand where others are & they true need; saying only the positive and avoiding confronting when necessary. Acts 14:22

Giving – persons gifted in the area of giving have the ability to give material goods and financial resources with joy so that the needs of the Lord's work are met. They often can discern wise investments and usually are effective money managers. They want to give quietly without recognition and are encouraged when they know needs are being met and prayers are being answered. These persons are more likely to give at the Lord's promptings than at human appeals. They have the ability to see financial needs others may overlook. If you scored high in this area, you should consider prayerfully what ministries of the church to support with your finances and how your example can motivate others to follow the Lord's leadership in their giving. Cautions: guard against greed; not forget to esteem their gift; forgetting the church's agenda is determined by the leaders & not the giver. I Corinthians 8:3-4

Helps – Persons gifted in the area are motivated by a desire to further the church's ministry by meeting the needs of others, especially those in leadership positions. They enjoy giving immediate help to key individuals in order to relieve them of their financial burdens and responsibilities. While these persons are willing to do whatever is needed, they are motivated more by a desire to provide assistance than by a desire to accomplish a task. If you scored high in this area, you should consider being involved in ministry in which you can provide assistance to someone in a leadership role to enable them to be more effective than they would be without you. Cautions: not forget to esteem their gift, difficult saying "no"; neglecting the priority of leadership's agenda. Romans 16:1-2

Hospitality – Persons gifted in the area of hospitality have the ability to make guests feel comfortable and at home. They have a desire to provide a warm welcome to guests, whether in a ministry or social setting. They often delight in opening their homes to individuals or groups and often look for opportunities to use their gift to minister to others. If you scored high in this area, you should consider being involved in a ministry where you can use your strengths to help make others in the church feel at home. Cautions: viewing gift as simply entertainment only; neglecting to ask God's guidance on who to seek & serve; putting pressure on their own families by inviting others into their homes. Hebrews 13:1-2

Leadership – Persons gifted in this area of leadership have the ability to lead others toward spiritual growth. They often are considered visionary and have the ability to set goals and motivate others toward accomplishing the goals. They usually have the ability to communicate effectively to large groups of people. These persons are often chosen for leadership positions because of their ability to accomplish objectives. While giftedness in leadership is similar to giftedness in administration, persons gifted in leadership are more concerned with the "big picture" than with the details of accomplishing tasks. If you scored high in this area you should consider being involved in an area of ministry in which you can use your strengths to lead others in accomplishing the church's measurable and non-measurable goals. (Non-measurable goals are objectives such as spiritual growth, atmosphere, and attitudes.) Cautions: rushing relational credibility critical for their effectiveness; not valuing servant leadership; forgetting that others can use this gift that are not in leadership. Hebrews 13:17

Mercy – Persons gifted in the area of mercy have immediate compassion for those who are suffering physically, spiritually, or emotionally. They derive great joy from meeting the needs of others and often attract people who are in distress. These persons usually need friendships in which there is deep communication and mutual commitment. They have the ability to draw out the feelings of others and are willing to be vulnerable to hurts, both directly and from feeling the hurts of others. they prefer to remove the causes of hurts rather than to look for spiritual benefits from them. Persons gifted in mercy have a tendency to avoid confrontation and firmness. They often close their spirit to those whom they feel are overly harsh or critical. If you scored high in this area, you should consider being involved in an area of ministry that enables you to minister to those who are hurting and who need the sensitivity you have to offer. Cautions: rescuing others from pain may be hindering God's work; becoming angry or defensive with the source of their pain; feeling unappreciated. Luke 10:33-34

Prophecy – Persons gifted in the area of prophecy have the ability to proclaim God's truth without compromise. They have strong convictions and expect others to have similar convictions. They need to express themselves verbally, especially about right and wrong. These persons may be quick to make judgments of others and quick to speak their opinions. They possess an unusual ability to discern other's sincerity and may be painfully direct when correcting others. They are persuasive in defining right and wrong and are persistent in expressing their feelings about the need for change. If you scored high in this area, you should look for a ministry area in which you can challenge others to live by God's standards as set forth in His Word. Cautions: not speaking with love & compassion; pride that can be demanding or discouraging the Spirit; discernment & scripture must support prophecy. I Corinthians 14:3

Service – Persons gifted in the area of service have the ability to perform any task with joy that benefits others and meets practical needs. They may have a tendency to disregard personal health and comfort to serve others. They often have difficulty saying no when asked to serve. These persons often have an affinity for details and appreciate having clear instructions. They enjoy the process of serving as much as the end result and derive satisfaction from being with others who are serving. If you scored high in this area, you should consider being involved in an area of ministry in which your strengths of faithfulness and attention to detail can be utilized. This gift is similar to Helps & Mercy. Cautions: not forget to esteem their gift, difficult saying "no"; neglecting the priority of leadership's agenda. Mark 10:45

Shepherding – Persons gifted in the area of shepherding have the unique ability to take responsibility for the long term spiritual growth of a group of believers. They see guiding, feeding and protecting a flock of Christ's followers as their responsibility. They are motivated by a desire to see those under them enjoying spiritual health and growth. If you scored high in this area, you should look for an area of ministry where discipleship is emphasized and in which you can guide others to greater spiritual maturity. Cautions: God will judge those who neglect or abuse their responsibilities;

may be difficult to say "no"; some you shepherd may grow beyond your own ability & should be allowed to do so. I Peter 5:2-3

Teaching – Persons gifted in the area of teaching have the ability to explain God's truth so that others can understand and apply it in their lives. They have the desire and ability to research and present truth in an organized, systematic fashion. They are alert to details and place great emphasis on accuracy. These persons are motivated by the desire to learn and share knowledge with others. They believe strongly in the importance of teaching as a basic foundation on which the church grows and remains faithful. If you scored high in this area, you should consider being involved in a ministry in which you can challenge others with Bible truths that you have discovered in your personal studies. Cautions: pride from their knowledge & understanding; becoming too detailed and not providing practical application; their spirituality is not based on acquiring more knowledge. Acts 28:30-31

Creative Communication – Persons gifted in the area of creative communication have the ability to communicate God's truth through a variety of art forms. They creatively develop and use artistic skills such as music, drama, photography, writing, art, etc. They enjoy using fresh, creative, and unconventional ways to express the message of Christ. Cautions: becoming overly sensitive and not able to receive constructive criticism; making the art's the main focus and not using it for the God's glory and the benefit of others; they need to guard against ego and work at being a team player. Exodus 31:3-5

Wisdom – Persons gifted in the area of wisdom have the ability to apply practically and effectively to meet a need in specific situations. They are able to foresee consequences and determine next steps. They understand how to meet the needs of others, the ability to come up with solutions in the midst of conflict and confusion, able to apply spiritual truth in specific and practical ways. Cautions: not sharing this gift with others, allowing others to depend on them instead of on God, being impatient with others who do not have same gift. Proverbs 9:9, 10:8

Ministry Opportunities within the local church

Lead Pastor
Assistant/Administration Pastor
Youth Pastor/Director
Children's Pastor/Director

Church Admin Assistant

Deacons/Elders

Trustees

Treasurer

Safety & Security Director

Head Usher, Ushers

Sunday School Superintendent
Adult Sunday School
Children's Sunday School

Sunday School Teachers
Small Group Leaders
Bible Study Leaders/Teachers

Choir Director
Choir & special music

Worship Leader
Worship Team (musicians, singers)

Nursery Director
Nursery workers
Children's programs
Children's choir, drama
Jr. High programs
High School programs
College Ministry

Singles Ministry

Women's Ministry

Men's Ministry

50+ Ministry

Media Team
Web site Administrator
Library/Resource Center

Counseling Ministry

Fellowship Ministry

Visitation Director (hospital, shut-ins, visitors, greeters)

Special Needs

Funerals Coordinator

Flowers & Decorating

Community Outreach (local nursing homes, food pantry, shelters, etc.)

Mission Trips

Baptism Coordinator

Wedding Coordinator

Custodian

Facilities Maintenance

Glossary

ARMOR OF GOD
Spiritual protection that God provides every believer (salvation, faith, righteousness, the Word of God, etc.)

BEGOTTEN
Unique; One of a kind

BELIEVER
A follower of Christ; person who has accepted Jesus Christ as their Lord & Savior (their forgiver and leader)

BLOOD OF JESUS CHRIST
He shed His blood on the cross for the salvation of mankind

BODY OF CHRIST
All believers in Jesus Christ; also known as the church, the Bride of Christ

BORN AGAIN
A spiritual rebirth (salvation); the process of accepting Christ as Savior, receiving of a new nature (His Spirit) and the promise of eternal life

BRIDE OF CHRIST
All the believers; local and universal

BRIDEGROOM
The Lord Jesus Christ

DAY OF THE LORD
The return of Christ to the earth; time of judgment and wrath of God on the earth; heaven and earth will pass away (II Peter 3:10)

DEATH
End of the physical body; spiritual death is the separation from God for eternity

FLESH
The physical, the sin nature, the old man

GRACE
God's favor and goodness; grace is God giving what we do not deserve

GREAT TRIBULATION
The second half (3 ½ years) of the tribulation period (characterized by God's judgments, wars, plagues and much suffering on the earth)

GREAT WHITE THRONE JUDGMENT
Judgment of the unbelievers

GOSPEL
The good news of the death, burial and resurrection of Jesus Christ; it proclaims God's love and salvation to all who believe by faith

JESUS CHRIST
God in the flesh, the second person in the Trinity; fully God (deity) and fully man (humanity)

JUDGMENT
God rendering rewards or punishment to every man according to his deeds (for the obedience or breaking of His holy law)

JUDGMENT SEAT OF CHRIST
Judgment of believers; not of sin (that was covered by the blood of Christ on the cross) but the receiving of rewards and crowns

JUSTICE
Getting what we deserve (judgment for sin)

LAMB'S BOOK OF LIFE
Book that holds the names of all believers; God puts the names of all those who have trusted in Jesus Christ as Savior

MERCY
God withholding from us what we deserve (His judgment for our sins)

MILLENNIUM
The 1000 year reign of Christ upon the earth (after His second coming)

RAPTURE
When Christ snatches believers (the church) to be with Him; not to be confused with the second coming of Christ upon the earth

REPENT
To turn and head in the opposite direction; true repentance requires remorse, a forsaking of sin and a change of direction

RESURRECTION OF JESUS CHRIST
The bodily return of Christ from the dead

SALVATION
A free gift from God; the forgiveness of sins, His Spirit indwelling us and a promise of eternal life; a transfer from the kingdom of darkness to the kingdom of light

SATAN
Also known as the devil, Beast, Dragon, Serpent of old, the accuser of the brethren, the enemy of God and the believer

SECOND COMING OF CHRIST
Christ return to the earth, this time as the Judge and King

SIN
Missing the mark of perfection, in word, deed, thought, attitude or motive. The breaking of God's commandments

SON OF GOD
Jesus Christ (speaks of His deity); fully God

SON OF MAN
Jesus Christ (speaks of His humanity); God in the flesh

SPIRIT FILLED
Believers are to be controlled by the Holy Spirit; under the influence

SPIRITUAL GIFTS
Set of abilities given by God to every believer to use in serving Him within the local church

SPIRITUAL WARFARE
The spiritual battle between a believer and the forces of darkness (Satan and his demons), the flesh and the world

STEWARD
The believer; put in charge of all that God has entrusted to him (time, talents, resources)

THE CHURCH
A body of believers (local or universal)

TITHING
Giving of our financial resources to further the cause of Christ

TRIBULATION
The seven year period (after the rapture of the church); reign of the Anti-Christ and the judgment/wrath of God upon the earth

TRINITY
Godhead – the Father, Son and Holy Spirit

UNBELIEVER
Those who have not put faith in (have rejected) Jesus Christ; whose names

are not written in the Lamb's Book of Life

WITNESSING
A believer sharing their faith in Jesus Christ with someone else; sharing the Gospel (the death, burial and resurrection of Christ)

WORLD
Society and today's value system; the culture we live in

About the Author

Doris Homan has been actively participating in women's ministries since the mid 1990's in the capacity of teaching Bible studies, leading small groups, speaking at women's events, one-on-one discipleship, and Christian counseling.

She resides with her husband John in Cincinnati, Ohio. They have three grown children and eight grandchildren. A graduate of the University of Cincinnati with a degree in Business, she is an executive assistant to the president of a private aviation company.

Made in the USA
Middletown, DE
18 January 2022